Everything You Always Wanted to Know About TRUMP LEADS And Were Not Afraid to Ask.

by George Rosenkranz

D1330126

Published by
Devyn Press, Inc.
Louisville, Kentucky

Cover by Bonnie Baron Pollack

Printed in the United States of America

Devyn Press, Inc.
151 Thierman Lane
Louisville, KY 40207

ISBN 0-910791-49-X

To Edith, Bobby, Jerry, Ricky and Heather,
who have inspired me in my dedication to the beauty of bridge
and in my belief that this game is a delightful form of art
everyone can enjoy.

Foreword

Imagine my surprise when George Rosenkranz called and asked me to write the foreword to his latest work, a book on opening trump leads!

Didn't George know that I had only written one other foreword before? Hadn't he ever heard of my generosity on opening lead?

Without mentioning any of this to George, I accepted. I did the right thing. It's a great book. It is well written and it deals with a topic that has been accorded little or no attention in the literature. Best of all, the book is loaded with striking example hands from actual competition.

You are always given the West hand, the bidding with explanations, and asked what you would lead. As you begin to absorb the principles laid down in the book, you are almost forced to realize how important it is to try to form a picture of the opponents' distribution before plunking that telltale opening lead on the table.

After you have carefully formed a picture, lead a trump! Just kidding. Although many of the examples are clearly slanted toward a trump lead, you are also told in so many words when a trump lead can be disastrous.

Another bonus: After you have made your brilliant (trump) opening lead, you are frequently shown the dummy and the hand is presented to you as a defensive problem. You get to match wits with the likes of Garozzo, etc.

Dr. Rosenkranz has tackled a tough subject, has presented a clear-cut method of analyzing the whys and wherefores of the opening trump lead, and, in my opinion, has hit the bull's-eye.

Personally, I don't think I am going to be quite so generous on opening leads anymore. Thanks, George.

Eddie Kantar
Los Angeles

Acknowledgments

Many people helped in the preparation of this book. I would particularly like to thank:

The American Contract Bridge League for its permission to use articles originally published in the *Bulletin*.

Phillip Alder for invaluable help in the preparation of the manuscript.

Dick Frey, Alan Truscott, Tannah Hirsch and Eddie Wold for constructive discussion and continuous encouragement.

Beatriz Coarasa for technical production assistance.

Contents

Introduction

In the modern game, bidding has become more important than card-play. This is because card-play techniques have been so well analyzed in bridge literature that nowadays players from countries normally considered weak in a bridge-playing sense are able to handle dummy-play with commendable competence. So reaching the right contract has become the primary aim of most top-level players. If you are always in the correct spot, you will never lose a match. But the lower you travel down the echelons of the game, the more important card-play and defense become. And even at the highest levels, defense still counts for a lot because bidding is not perfect. Of course, the declarer enjoys a considerable edge because he can see all his side's assets, but in an effort to counterbalance this, the defenders make the opening lead. And if you always find the best opening lead, you will be extremely tough to beat.

Whole books have been devoted to opening leads, but perhaps the most controversial aspect of the subject is the trump lead. Many years ago S. J. ('Skid') Simon wrote a classic book, *Why You Lose at Bridge,* but it included one piece of bad advice. He suggested: "When in doubt, lead trumps."

At the other end of the spectrum is the cynical observation of one of America's world champions: "Never lead trumps . . . unless it's right!"

In spite of some useful but widely-scattered information written by prominent bridge authorities in textbooks and encyclopedias, no wonder the earnest average player feels lost. When should one lead a trump?

In a conversation with the great Italian player, Benito Garozzo, he stated: "It is too difficult to postulate general rules. Each case is different and requires delicate judgment." His opinion supports my conviction: you should lead a trump *not* when in *doubt,* but when you have a good *reason* for it. And it is important to bear in mind that when there is a killing lead, it will be in the trump suit far less often than in a side suit.

With that thought held firmly in mind, this book is an attempt to tackle the difficult subject of trump leads in the hope that some of the research and analysis I have undertaken will help the average player to sharpen his own judgment — and add extra weight to Bobby Nail's complimentary comment to me a short while ago that I am making life more difficult for the pros as I am teaching everyone not only how to bid and play but also now how to defend.

The skeleton of the material assembled here comes from a series of articles I wrote for the A.C.B.L. *Bulletin,* but the liberty of more space in a book has permitted me to expand the ideas and include many more example hands from actual play. Also, unless otherwise stated, the bidding will be along the lines of a system including five-card majors, a strong notrump and weak two-bids.

And now on to the first chapter with its seemingly paradoxical title!

Chapter 1

WHEN NOT TO LEAD TRUMPS

Wich puts me in mind o' man as killed hisself on
principle, wich o' course you've heard on, sir.

SAM WELLER IN PICKWICK PAPERS, CHARLES DICKENS

This seems to be an exact reversal of the purpose of this book,
but if we have a clear idea of when to reject a trump lead, it
will be easier to bring into focus our main subject.

Before formulating some general rules, though, I feel I must
emphasize a most important piece of advice: *Listen to the bidding and think before doing anything.*

There are three situations in which *usually* a trump should
not be led:

    A.   If it may cost you a trick

    B.   If it may cost your partner a trick

    C.   If it is more important to do something else

Let us consider them in turn.

A. This is the simplest of all the cases. I am sure you would
not consider leading away from a useful trump holding like
KJ(x), Qx(xx) or Jxxx, presenting declarer with a free finesse
or costing yourself a trick (unless making a deceptive lead,
which we will consider in Chapter 5).

B. Leading from Jx or Jxx is also often bad. If your partner
is holding an honor, you may have lost a trick which belonged
to your side, as illustrated in the following diagrams:

1.

	Dummy	
	K 10 9 4	
You		Partner
J 6 5		Q 8
	Declarer	
	A 7 3 2	

2.

	Dummy	
	Q 10 7 4	
You		Partner
J 6 5		K 8
	Declarer	
	A 9 3 2	

In either case, if you lead a trump and declarer guesses correctly, your side's trump trick will have disappeared.

Even leading away from 10xx may sometimes cost a trick.

3.

	Dummy	
	Q 9 3	
You		Partner
10 6 5		K 8 4
	Declarer	
	A J 7 2	

4.

	Dummy	
	J 9 3	
You		Partner
10 6 5		Q 8 4
	Declarer	
	A K 7 2	

Real-life hands of this type from world championships are rare, but board 46 of the North America-France Bermuda Bowl encounter in Buenos Aires in 1961 provides such an example.

Dealer: South
Vulnerable: None

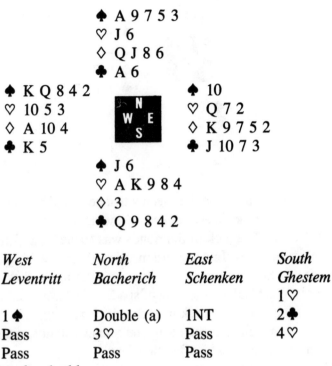

♠ A 9 7 5 3
♡ J 6
◊ Q J 8 6
♣ A 6

♠ K Q 8 4 2
♡ 10 5 3
◊ A 10 4
♣ K 5

♠ 10
♡ Q 7 2
◊ K 9 7 5 2
♣ J 10 7 3

♠ J 6
♡ A K 9 8 4
◊ 3
♣ Q 9 8 4 2

West	North	East	South
Leventritt	Bacherich	Schenken	Ghestem
			1♡
1♠	Double (a)	1NT	2♣
Pass	3♡	Pass	4♡
Pass	Pass	Pass	

(a) Penalty double

Peter Leventritt, trying to make a 'safe' lead, unfortunately selected the three of hearts, and the declarer, Pierre Ghestem, managed to make his contract. He played low from dummy and captured East's queen with his ace. A diamond went to dummy's queen and East's king, and Howard Schenken switched to his singleton spade. Dummy won with the ace, a diamond was ruffed, dummy reentered with a trump to the jack, another diamond ruffed and the king of hearts cashed. That left this position with the declarer needing four more tricks:

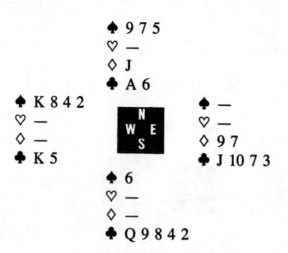

Declarer led his spade, and seeing that he would be endplayed if he won the trick, West ducked, allowing dummy's seven to win the trick. The jack of diamonds was cashed and followed by the ace of clubs. In desperation, West threw the king under the ace, so South's queen of clubs was the tenth trick.

If only West had led the king of spades, declarer would have been destined to lose a trick in each suit. And at the other table the American pair, Norman Kay and Sidney Silodor, made exactly nine tricks in 2♡ after that lead.

Even a seemingly safe trump lead such as the ten from 1094 may result in a serious loss, as occurred on the following deal.

Dealer: South
Vulnerable: None

```
                  ♠ 2
                  ♡ K Q 6
                  ◇ K Q 9 6 4
                  ♣ A J 5 3
  ♠ 5                          ♠ K J 8 7 6 3
  ♡ 9 8 5 4 2        N         ♡ 10 3
  ◇ A 5 3 2       W   E        ◇ 10 8 7
  ♣ 10 9 4          S          ♣ Q 8
                  ♠ A Q 10 9 4
                  ♡ A J 7
                  ◇ J
                  ♣ K 7 6 2
```

West	North	East	South
			1 ♠
Pass	2 ◇	Pass	3 ♣
Pass	4NT	Pass	5 ♡
Pass	6 ♣	Pass	Pass
Pass			

South received the ten of clubs lead and ran it round to his king. Since it was most unlikely that West was leading away from the queen, the only way to avoid a trump loser was to try to drop her highness. When this worked, the declarer got the diamonds going and made his slam. Left to his own devices after a non-trump lead, the declarer would have had no reason not to take the trump finesse and so would have gone down — which is precisely what happened at the other table.

Leading away from Kxx or Axx is less likely to cost, though it is possible to lose a potential trick if partner holds the jack; and you will have saved the declarer a guess if the trump suit is distributed in either of these ways:

5.
	Dummy	
	Q 9 7 6	
You		Partner
K 5 3		J 4
	Declarer	
	A 10 8 2	

6.
	Dummy	
	K 8 5 4	
You		Partner
A 6 3		J 2
	Declarer	
	Q 10 9 7	

Except in certain circumstances that we will cover later, *do not lead a singleton trump.*

Obviously, if the singleton is an honor, you may have helped declarer to solve his problem in the suit — unless he thinks you have made a tricky lead such as the jack from queen-jack doubleton.

This is a possible layout:

7.
	Dummy	
	A 10 7 6	
You		Partner
J		Q 8 4
	Declarer	
	K 9 5 3 2	

And here are two positions where leading a singleton honor saves declarer a headache.

8.

                Dummy
                Q 10 6 5

You   *Partner*
J   K 7 3

                Declarer
                A 9 8 4 2

9.

                Dummy
                K 9 6 5

You   *Partner*
A   J 8 3

                Declarer
                Q 10 7 4 2

Also, if declarer has a two-way finesse for the queen, leading your singleton low trump will earn declarer's gratitude but merit partner's ire.

10.

                Dummy
                K J 10 4

You   *Partner*
6   Q 8 3

                Declarer
                A 9 7 5 2

On other occasions you will make life easy for declarer.

11.

                Dummy
                Q 10 6 4

You   *Partner*
5   K J 3

                Declarer
                A 9 8 7 2

12.

	Dummy	
	Q 9 6	
You		*Partner*
5		J 10 7 3
	Declarer	
	A K 8 4 2	

In 11, the percentage play for only one loser is to lay down the ace and follow by leading low to the queen. This time that line produces two tricks for the defense — unless you led your trump!

In 12, declarer would have no reason (unless being guided from the bidding) to play for anything other than a 3-2 break. But after a trump lead he will almost certainly pick up the suit for no losers.

The above set of card combinations is obviously not complete, but hopefully it has impressed upon you the point about undesirable trump leads.

C. There are many reasons why you should not be leading a trump other than the inherent risk of costing your side a trick in the suit. Five are:

    a.   Partner has instructed you to lead a particular suit
    b.   The need to establish or cash a trick in a side suit
    c.   The desire to give partner a ruff, or to achieve one for yourself
    d.   To destroy declarer's communications
    e.   To force declarer

a. This will usually be via a lead-directing double. The original conception came from the late, great Theodore Lightner with his double of freely-bid slams.

For example, with both sides vulnerable, you, West, hold

♠ 6 4   ♡ 10 8 6 4 3 2   ◊ K Q 10   ♣ 5 3

The dealer on your right opens 7♠ and your partner doubles! What is your opening lead?

East is saying that he has an unexpected void somewhere in his hand and is hoping his partner can find it with his lead so that an immediate ruff will defeat the slam. In this case West should lead a heart, expecting the full deal to be something like this:

Dealer: South
Vulnerable: Both

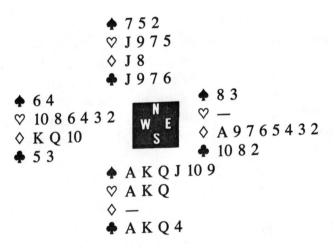

```
                    ♠ 7 5 2
                    ♡ J 9 7 5
                    ◊ J 8
                    ♣ J 9 7 6
   ♠ 6 4                        ♠ 8 3
   ♡ 10 8 6 4 3 2               ♡ —
   ◊ K Q 10                     ◊ A 9 7 6 5 4 3 2
   ♣ 5 3                        ♣ 10 8 2
                    ♠ A K Q J 10 9
                    ♡ A K Q
                    ◊ —
                    ♣ A K Q 4
```

As you can see, without the heart ruff at trick one, declarer can claim 13 tricks.

Occasionally this principle can be used at a lower level. With neither side vulnerable, you are West holding

♠ 10   ♡ A J 10 8 7 3   ◊ 8 7 2   ♣ 10 9 6

The bidding is competitive and includes an unusual transfer bid:

West	North	East	South
			1NT (a)
2♡ (b)	4♢ (c)	Pass	4♠
Pass	Pass	Double	Pass
Pass	Pass		

(a) 13-15 points
(b) Sporting!
(c) A transfer to 4♠

What is your opening lead?

Despite the fact that you have made such a weak overcall, partner will not double 4♠ in the hope that you will be producing two or three defensive tricks. It is more profitable to play a double of a freely-bid game like this as lead-directing. Start with the ace of hearts and play a second heart, confident that partner will ruff it. (If he does not, he had better produce three tricks himself!)

This was the full deal:

Dealer: South
Vulnerable: None

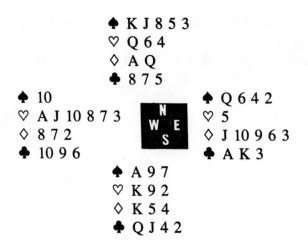

                    ♠ K J 8 5 3
                    ♡ Q 6 4
                    ◇ A Q
                    ♣ 8 7 5
    ♠ 10   ♠ Q 6 4 2
    ♡ A J 10 8 7 3   ♡ 5
    ◇ 8 7 2   ◇ J 10 9 6 3
    ♣ 10 9 6   ♣ A K 3
                    ♠ A 9 7
                    ♡ K 9 2
                    ◇ K 5 4
                    ♣ Q J 4 2

At the time West led a diamond, an unwise choice after partner had failed to double 4♦. Declarer won in the dummy and led the jack of spades. This won the trick, and when the singleton ten appeared, declarer happily continued with a spade to the nine, cashed the ace of spades, returned to dummy with a diamond and drew the last trump. When a club was led from the dummy, East went up with the king and switched to his singleton heart. West decided to duck this, and so declarer was able to make an overtrick by playing another club. In fact East won with the ace and exited with a club, but declarer had two minor-suit winners upon which to pitch dummy's heart losers.

There are other positions when it will normally be right to make the lead partner has indicated rather than to start with a trump. These include when he has made an overcall or has doubled a cuebid or Blackwood response; but if we give examples of all these routine situations, we will never get on to the chapters about trump leads themselves!

b. Alan Truscott, in his column in *The New York Times*, gave this interesting example: Sitting West with neither side vulnerable, you hold

♠ Q 9 7 4 2   ♡ Q 8 5 4   ♦ 8 5   ♣ 10 6

and the bidding proceeds:

West	North	East	South
			1♦
Pass	2♣	Pass	3♦
Pass	4NT	Pass	5♡
Pass	6♣	Pass	6NT
Pass	Pass	Double	Pass
Pass	7♦	Pass	Pass
Pass			

What is your lead?

At the table West made the 'safe' lead of a trump and declarer tabled his cards immediately.

West was guilty of failing to think. For his double of 6 NT, East had to have the ace-king of spades or hearts, and so West should have tried to guess which major to lead.

He may not have picked the right suit, but at least he had a 50 percent chance.

This was the actual full deal:

Dealer: South
Vulnerable: None

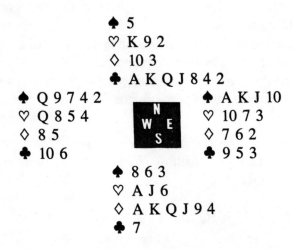

                    ♠ 5
                    ♡ K 9 2
                    ◊ 10 3
                    ♣ A K Q J 8 4 2
    ♠ Q 9 7 4 2   ♠ A K J 10
    ♡ Q 8 5 4   ♡ 10 7 3
    ◊ 8 5   ◊ 7 6 2
    ♣ 10 6   ♣ 9 5 3
                    ♠ 8 6 3
                    ♡ A J 6
                    ◊ A K Q J 9 4
                    ♣ 7

North's imaginative bid, keeping the person who obviously held the ace-king of spades off the lead, converted a penalty of 700 into a profit of 1440. (Needless to say, East's double of 6 NT was foolish.)

During the 1981 Mexican Nationals another typical case occured where an attacking lead was needed before declarer could take his discards. I held

    ♠ 10 9   ♡ A 8 4   ◊ Q 9 8 6   ♣ 10 9 6 2

and the bidding proceeded:

West	North	East	South
			1 ♠
Pass	2NT (a)	Pass	3 ♡
Pass	4 ♡	Pass	4NT (b)
Pass	5 ♡ (c)	Pass	6 ♡
Pass	Pass	Pass	

(a) 13-15 balanced
(b) Roman Key Card Blackwood
(c) Two of the key cards (the four aces and the king of hearts) but not the queen of hearts

It was easy to visualize that if I gave up the trump ace, declarer's spade suit would furnish a parking place for a few of dummy's minor-suit cards. Thus an aggressive lead in one of the minors was mandatory.

As to which minor, I am sure you will reason along these lines: Following the Blackwood auction, partner cannot be expected to hold an ace, and in order to defeat the contract, I need partner to hold either one card in diamonds, the king, or two cards in clubs, the king and queen.

This makes the diamond lead the correct choice; and it turned out that I had found the way to sink the contract when the full deal proved to be:

Dealer: South
Vulnerable: North-South

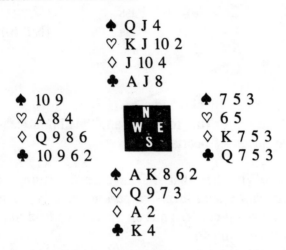

```
              ♠ Q J 4
              ♡ K J 10 2
              ◊ J 10 4
              ♣ A J 8
  ♠ 10 9                        ♠ 7 5 3
  ♡ A 8 4          N            ♡ 6 5
  ◊ Q 9 8 6     W     E         ◊ K 7 5 3
  ♣ 10 9 6 2       S            ♣ Q 7 5 3
              ♠ A K 8 6 2
              ♡ Q 9 7 3
              ◊ A 2
              ♣ K 4
```

After winning the diamond lead with the ace, declarer tried a desperate finesse of the jack of clubs and wound up two down.

Was the diamond lead risky? Not at all: If partner does not hold the king of diamonds, there are no diamond tricks coming the defense's way.

This time you hold

♠ K J 6 5   ♡ K J 8 5 4   ◊ J 10   ♣ 4 2

and with only the opponents vulnerable, you hear this auction:

West	North	East	South
	2♣ (a)	Pass	2◊ (b)
Pass	2♡ (c)	Pass	5◊
Pass	5♡	Pass	6◊
Pass	Pass	Pass	

(a) Precision; natural with five or more clubs and at most 15 points
(b) Relay asking for more information
(c) Second suit

What is your lead?

The more unusual the bidding, the more informative it may be. Here you can read North for five hearts and six clubs, and South for a long diamond suit, probably with four spades as well as he bothered to use the 2 ◊ relay before blasting to 5 ◊. Also, it is likely North is void in diamonds for his attempt to improve the contract — he can hardly be cuebidding in the hunt for a grand slam! All this, of course, leaves you with a most unattractive lead. Which is your poison?

At the table the player made the poor decision to lead the jack of diamonds. In other circumstances it would not be such a bad choice because all the side-suit leads do seem to be risky, but here a trump lead is even more fraught with danger as it will take any finesses for declarer, and South probably does not hold solid diamonds as he went past 3 NT.

This proved to be the full deal:

Dealer: North
Vulnerable: North-South

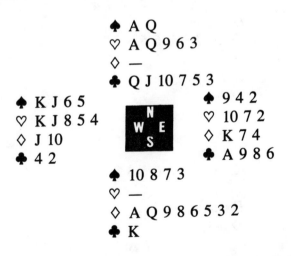

```
              ♠ A Q
              ♡ A Q 9 6 3
              ◊ —
              ♣ Q J 10 7 5 3
♠ K J 6 5                      ♠ 9 4 2
♡ K J 8 5 4        N           ♡ 10 7 2
◊ J 10          W     E        ◊ K 7 4
♣ 4 2              S           ♣ A 9 8 6
              ♠ 10 8 7 3
              ♡ —
              ◊ A Q 9 8 6 5 3 2
              ♣ K
```

Declarer won the first trick with the queen of diamonds, cashed the ace, finessed the queen of spades, discarded the king of clubs on the ace of hearts, ruffed out the ace of clubs and conceded a trump trick, his two spade losers going on dummy's club winners.

I think the winning club lead is difficult to find. However, a major-suit lead leaves the declarer with a guess in the trump suit which he is likely to get wrong. Suppose that West leads a spade. The queen is finessed in the dummy, the king of clubs thrown on the ace of hearts and the queen of clubs led for a ruffing finesse.

Let us assume first of all that East puts up his ace immediately. Declarer ruffs it and cashes the ace of diamonds, noting the fall of, say, the ten from West. Now the declarer is not sure how the trump suit is divided, but if he is to make the contract, he knows it must be one of the following:

1.
	Dummy	
	◇ —	
West		*East*
◇ J 10		◇ K 7 4
	Declarer	
	◇ A Q 9 8 6 5 3 2	

2.
	Dummy	
	◇ —	
West		*East*
◇ K 10		◇ J 7 4
	Declarer	
	◇ A Q 9 8 6 5 3 2	

3.
	Dummy	
	◇ —	
West		*East*
◇ J 10 7		◇ K 4
	Declarer	
	◇ A Q 9 8 6 5 3 2	

In the third case, West must drop one of his honors; a mandatory false-card situation to give declarer a losing option. (More will be said about this in the chapter on deceptive trump leads.) In two cases declarer must lead low on the second round to succeed, whereas only in the first layout is it right to continue with the queen. That already shows why a good declarer will get the actual hand wrong. But there is an extra percentage in favor of the losing play, if that does not sound too paradoxical. By applying the Principle of Restricted Choice we find that the second position is more likely than the first. If we assume West will drop equal cards (the jack and ten) with equal regularity, when he drops specifically the ten we may make the assumption he does not hold the jack as well because half the time he would have played that card, whereas without it his play is forced.

Now consider the difference if East does not play his ace of clubs on either of the first two club leads. Declarer discards two spades, ruffs a heart and still has to guess the trump suit. However, if he *knows* West has a doubleton club (not so unlikely from East's play), he can no longer succeed in the third layout above because East will win the second round of trumps and play a club to promote West's remaining diamond honor. And as the second position is more likely than the first, declarer will still probably continue with a low trump on the second round and go down.

c. In the Mexican Trials of 1979 I held

♠ J 10 9 3   ♡ A   ◇ A 9 6 2   ♣ 6 5 4 2

My opponents bid as follows:

West	North	East	South
			1 ♡
Pass	2 ♣	Pass	3 ♣
Pass	3 ♡	Pass	4 ♡
Pass	Pass	Pass	

What is your lead?

I reasoned that the opponents probably held an eight-card club fit and therefore partner was short in the suit. Also, he should have two or three trumps as I was short in that department. Holding two entries in my hand, I led the two of clubs, hoping to give him one, two or even three ruffs, and at the same time indicating to partner that my entry was in diamonds rather than spades: It is not often one can make a suit preference signal with one's opening lead.

This was the full deal:

Dealer: South
Vulnerable: East-West

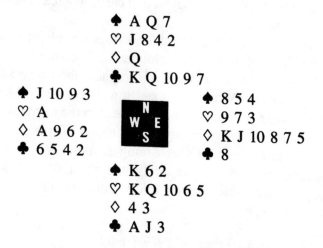

```
                    ♠ A Q 7
                    ♡ J 8 4 2
                    ◊ Q
                    ♣ K Q 10 9 7
   ♠ J 10 9 3                      ♠ 8 5 4
   ♡ A                  N          ♡ 9 7 3
   ◊ A 9 6 2         W   E         ◊ K J 10 8 7 5
   ♣ 6 5 4 2           S           ♣ 8
                    ♠ K 6 2
                    ♡ K Q 10 6 5
                    ◊ 4 3
                    ♣ A J 3
```

I felt happy with the outcome, but my partner was less pleased.

"Why didn't you double, George?" he demanded.

Momentarily I felt uncomfortable, but then it occurred to me that if North or South retreated to 5♣, it would require specific defense to defeat it. My partner would have to lead a heart to my ace, I would have to underlead my ace of diamonds and he would have to give me a heart ruff. Not impossible to find, but I asked my partner if he really would have preferred us to have been put to that test, or whether it was in fact easier to accept the straightforward defense against 4♡.

It rarely pays to make a penalty double after an uncontested auction unless you are sure you can deal with all other possible resting spots the opponents may try once you warn them they are in the wrong contract.

Visualizing partner's shortage is certainly more difficult than leading a singleton in the hope of obtaining a ruff. No example should be needed to illustrate this latter elementary situation, but this deal from a club game was amusing.

As West, you hold

♠ Q 9 6 4 3   ♡ 7 4 3   ◇ A   ♣ Q J 6 4

You hear the following simple auction:

West	North	East	South
			1♠
Pass	2♠	Pass	3♡
Pass	4♡	Pass	Pass
Pass			

What do you lead?

Of course, the defense is a cinch. You lead the ace of diamonds, and follow with the nine of spades, a suit preference signal. Partner ruffs and returns a diamond, but as declarer has a doubleton diamond, the cross-ruff yields a defensive total of only four tricks; though enough to defeat the contract.

A trump lead would have been less successful as the full deal was:

Dealer: South
Vulnerable: East-West

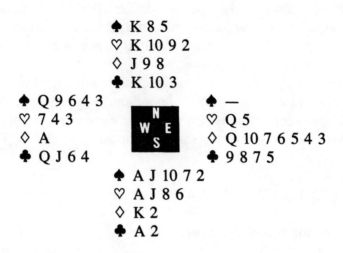

♠ K 8 5
♡ K 10 9 2
◇ J 9 8
♣ K 10 3

♠ Q 9 6 4 3
♡ 7 4 3
◇ A
♣ Q J 6 4

♠ —
♡ Q 5
◇ Q 10 7 6 5 4 3
♣ 9 8 7 5

♠ A J 10 7 2
♡ A J 8 6
◇ K 2
♣ A 2

Perhaps West was tempted to double here, but if South had then corrected to 4♠, probably West would have ended up a wiser and poorer man.

Still sitting West, you hold

♠ Q 9 6 3   ♡ J 6 4   ◇ K Q 10 8 2   ♣ A

and allow the unfavorable vulnerability to keep you out of an auction that proceeds:

West	North	East	South
			2♡
Pass	4♡	Pass	Pass
Pass			

What is your opening lead?

The actual West started down the wrong track when he led the king of diamonds. This was the full deal:

Dealer: South
Vulnerable: East-West

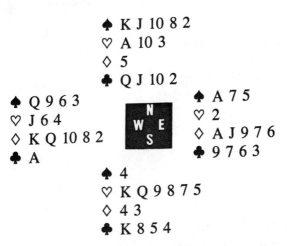

```
                ♠ K J 10 8 2
                ♡ A 10 3
                ◇ 5
                ♣ Q J 10 2
  ♠ Q 9 6 3                    ♠ A 7 5
  ♡ J 6 4          N           ♡ 2
  ◇ K Q 10 8 2   W   E         ◇ A J 9 7 6
  ♣ A              S           ♣ 9 7 6 3
                ♠ 4
                ♡ K Q 9 8 7 5
                ◇ 4 3
                ♣ K 8 5 4
```

East overtook at trick one and switched to a club. West won with his singleton ace and led a spade. How should declarer play from there?

In fact I was the declarer, and it was clear that East had the ace of spades, otherwise West would have made a bid over 2♡. But there was a good reason for putting up dummy's king of spades. If I finessed the ten and East had to win with the ace, he would have nothing else to do but switch back to clubs and maybe achieve the ruff they needed to defeat my contract. However, when I appeared to misguess by calling for the king, East tried to cash his partner's queen of spades. That allowed me to ruff, play the king of hearts to check the trumps were not 4-0, ruff my diamond loser in the dummy with the ten of hearts, cash the ace, ruff a spade to return to hand, draw the last trump and claim.

West, of course, should have led the ace of clubs, which would have clarified matters; and if East had assumed I could count the points, he might have worked out why I had apparently made an error in the spade suit. Finally, note that a trump lead, though not instantly fatal, makes life tough for East-West.

This time both sides are vulnerable, and you are surveying

♠ 10 9   ♡ K 8 7 6 4   ◊ A K J 7 6 2   ♣ —

The opponents' bidding goes:

West	North	East	South
			2♠ (a)
3◊	3♠	Pass	4♣
Pass	4♡	Pass	4♠
Pass	5♣	Pass	6♠
Pass	Pass	Pass	

(a) Strong, Acol-style two-bid

What is your opening lead?

One of the more common gambits in bridge is the underlead of a string of honors against a slam when holding a void in a side suit. Not all are successful (and those that are not tend to be quietly forgotten), but in this case Steen Møller, playing for Denmark against Turkey in the 1968 European Championship in Oslo, decided the risk was worth it and led the two of diamonds.

As you can guess, this proved to be the killing lead as the full deal was:

Dealer: South
Vulnerable: Both

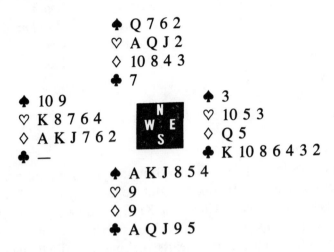

```
                    ♠ Q 7 6 2
                    ♡ A Q J 2
                    ◊ 10 8 4 3
                    ♣ 7
  ♠ 10 9                           ♠ 3
  ♡ K 8 7 6 4        N             ♡ 10 5 3
  ◊ A K J 7 6 2    W   E           ◊ Q 5
  ♣ —                 S            ♣ K 10 8 6 4 3 2
                    ♠ A K J 8 5 4
                    ♡ 9
                    ◊ 9
                    ♣ A Q J 9 5
```

When Møller's partner, Arne Pedersen, won the first trick with the queen of diamonds, he had no trouble working out the position and returned a club for his partner to ruff.

Of course, in this case declarer might not have made the slam if left to his own resources after two rounds of diamonds, but it is better from the defenders' point of view not to have to find out.

The following hand occurred during the 1979 Bermuda Bowl in Rio de Janeiro. With only your side vulnerable, you are holding

♠ 8 7 3   ♡ A J 9 7 2   ◊ —   ♣ A J 10 8 7

The auction proceeds:

West	North	East	South
Kuo	Passell	Huang	Brachman
1♡ (a)	Pass	3♡ (b)	4♠
Pass	Pass	Double	Pass
Pass	Pass		

(a) Precision
(b) Limit raise with at least four trumps

What is your opening lead?

It does not look right to lead a trump; trying for a diamond ruff seems much more productive. But the leap to game by South suggests a shapely hand. Che-hung Kuo, representing Taiwan, decided to play his partner for the king of hearts as part of his limit raise and led the nine of hearts, an unnecessarily high card as a suit preference signal for diamonds.

This proved to be the full deal:

Dealer: West
Vulnerable: East-West

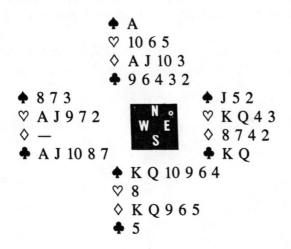

```
                    ♠ A
                    ♡ 10 6 5
                    ◊ A J 10 3
                    ♣ 9 6 4 3 2
   ♠ 8 7 3                        ♠ J 5 2
   ♡ A J 9 7 2      N             ♡ K Q 4 3
   ◊ —            W   E           ◊ 8 7 4 2
   ♣ A J 10 8 7     S             ♣ K Q
                    ♠ K Q 10 9 6 4
                    ♡ 8
                    ◊ K Q 9 6 5
                    ♣ 5
```

Patrick Huang won the first trick with the queen of hearts and led the two of diamonds as a suit preference signal of his own. Kuo ruffed and underled an ace for the second time. In this way he received a second ruff and defeated the contract.

That brilliant defense just reduced the loss on the board, however. This was the auction in the other room:

West	North	East	South
Kantar	Chen	Eisenberg	Tai
1♡	Pass	3♡	3♠
4♣	Pass	4♡	4♠
Pass	Pass	5♡	Pass
Pass	Double	Pass	Pass
Pass			

This contract rated to lose the first three spade tricks, but with North holding the singleton ace, Eddie Kantar was able to make his contract by drawing trumps, discarding dummy's spade losers on his clubs and ruffing a spade in the dummy. So the United States gained 13 International Matchpoints (IMPs).

A trump lead against 4♠ would not have been immediately fatal; and that was the choice of the West player representing Central American-Caribbean (a combined Panamanian and Venezuelan team) at another table who chose to pass as dealer and heard South open with 4♠ in fourth seat. However, when the declarer, Brazilian star Gabriel Chagas, led a club from the dummy, East did not find the killing diamond switch. He cashed a heart trick before reverting to clubs, so declarer took 11 tricks.

It is normally right to lead a trump when the declarer seems likely to be making his contract with ruffs in the dummy or hand (a dummy reversal) or by a cross-ruff. However, if you can see that you are either long in declarer's suit or short in dummy's and your side might be able to score an overruff, you should usually make a side-suit lead. If you start with a trump, there is a risk declarer will score a trump trick with a low spot-card and then to be able to take his ruff high to avoid the overruff.

Only the opponents are vulnerable and you are West, looking at

♠ 6   ♡ J 10 9 6 4 3   ◊ 9 4   ♣ K J 9 5

The auction proceeds:

West	North	East	South
2♡	2♠	Pass	3◊
Pass	4♡ (a)	Pass	4NT (b)
Pass	5♠ (c)	Pass	7◊
Pass	Pass	Pass	

(a) A splinter bid showing a singleton or void in hearts and diamond support
(b) Roman Key Card Blackwood
(c) Two key cards and the queen of diamonds

What is your opening lead?

Here you cannot be sure partner is short in hearts, but there is an inference he does not hold length in the suit because he did not raise hearts to suggest a save at the favorable vulnerability. So it is close between trying an aggressive side-suit lead and a passive trump.

This was the full deal:

Dealer: West
Vulnerable: North-South

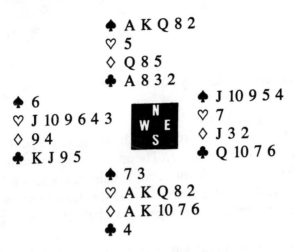

```
            ♠ A K Q 8 2
            ♡ 5
            ◊ Q 8 5
            ♣ A 8 3 2
♠ 6                          ♠ J 10 9 5 4
♡ J 10 9 6 4 3      N        ♡ 7
◊ 9 4            W     E      ◊ J 3 2
♣ K J 9 5           S        ♣ Q 10 7 6
            ♠ 7 3
            ♡ A K Q 8 2
            ◊ A K 10 7 6
            ♣ 4
```

Against a major-suit lead, declarer would probably draw trumps and play for the spades to break no worse than 4-2. To ruff a heart with the queen of diamonds and then finesse for the jack of trumps has less appeal.

After a club lead, a logical line is to win with the ace, draw two rounds of trumps from hand and start on the spades. Once more, defeat is the result.

However, if West leads a trump, the declarer will probably read the position and make the hand regardless of the spade break. If East plays the jack of diamonds at trick one, it is easy for declarer, so let us assume he withholds the honor. But now declarer will be able to win with the six, ruff a heart with the queen of diamonds and draw trumps.

For the last example in this section, only your side is vulnerable and you are looking at

♠ A 8   ♡ 10 8 4 3 2   ◊ J 8 7 6 3   ♣ A

The bidding goes:

West	North	East	South
		3♠	4♣ (a)
4♠	5♣	Pass	Pass
Pass			

(a) Fishbein: conventionally for take-out

What is your opening lead?

You can hope for tricks from your black-suit aces, but from where will a third trick come? The most likely possibility is from a red-suit ruff by partner. So should you guess a heart or diamond lead? Or it is better to lead the ace of spades and hope to be able to find the winning switch after seeing the dummy?

If you decided to do the latter, this is what you would have seen:

Dealer: East
Vulnerable: East-West

```
              ♠ 6 5 4
              ♡ K 9
              ◇ A 2
              ♣ Q 10 9 8 6 5
   ♠ A 8
   ♡ 10 8 4 3 2
   ◇ J 8 7 6 3
   ♣ A
```

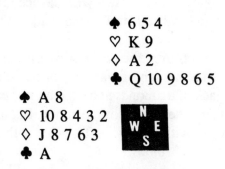

What do you lead at trick two?

Obviously the dummy suggests a diamond switch (and if you have discussed this situation with your partner, he might have given you a suit preference signal at trick one). Declarer is more likely to have four hearts and five diamonds for his take-out bid than five hearts and four diamonds.

That would have defeated the contract, but at the time Harry Merkel, an American expert of yesteryear, playing in a pair game in San Francisco, found an alternative and very imaginative play: at trick one he led the eight of spades! For his vulnerable preempt, partner could be expected to hold the king, and he knew which singleton he held.

The plan worked perfectly when the full deal proved to be:

Dealer: East
Vulnerable: East-West

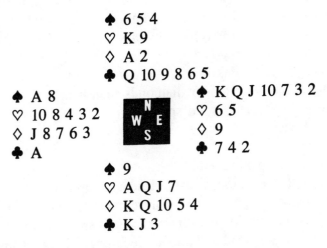

East won the first trick with the ten of spades, switched to the nine of diamonds, and received a diamond ruff at trick four.

d. You, West, hold the following hand at unfavorable vulnerability:

♠ J 10 9 6　　♡ K 6 5　　◇ 9　　♣ Q 10 8 4 3

and the auction proceeds:

West Théron	North Garozzo	East Desrousseaux	South Chiaradia
		Pass	1 ♡
Pass	2 ♠	Pass	3 ◇ (a)
Pass	3 ♠ (b)	Pass	4NT
Pass	5 ♠ (c)	Pass	5NT
Pass	6 ◇	Pass	7 ◇
Pass	Pass	Pass	

(a) Canapé showing longer diamonds than hearts
(b) Promises virtually solid spades
(c) Three aces

What is your opening lead?

At first glance, it looks best to lead a trump in order to give nothing away, but you should analyze more deeply. You know dummy is coming down with an excellent spade suit and two other aces. If you lead a diamond, declarer will draw trumps, set up the spades with a ruff, return to dummy and run the remaining spades to make his grand slam.

The actual West, Georges Théron, playing for France against Italy in the 1963 Bermuda Bowl, realized the necessity to dislodge dummy's entry; so he led the four of clubs. (If dummy held the aces of clubs and hearts, there would be no chance to defeat the contract.) This proved to be the most effective choice, the full hand being:

Dealer: East
Vulnerable: East-West

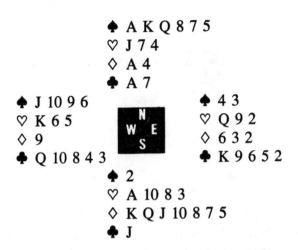

♠ A K Q 8 7 5
♡ J 7 4
◊ A 4
♣ A 7

♠ J 10 9 6
♡ K 6 5
◊ 9
♣ Q 10 8 4 3

♠ 4 3
♡ Q 9 2
◊ 6 3 2
♣ K 9 6 5 2

♠ 2
♡ A 10 8 3
◊ K Q J 10 8 7 5
♣ J

What an easy contract without a club lead! And Eugenio Chiaradia failed to make his grand slam after it.

He could have relied on a 3-3 spade break, which is a 35.5 percent chance; but in fact chose to go for the slightly more likely 2-2 diamond break — a 40.7 percent possibility. As you can see, the trumps did not divide and so he went down, East ruffing the third round of spades.

It is such an interesting hand, though, that we must not move on without considering it further. How should declarer play in 7◊ after a club lead?

A better line than those mentioned above is to play for spades to be 3-3 or the person with the long spades to have both the king-queen of hearts or any five hearts. Winning the first trick with the ace of clubs, declarer draws trumps, cashes the ace of hearts and plays off the rest of the trumps.

In fact with the actual layout this play does not work either; but the great French player-writer José le Dentu spotted that there is a way to bring home the contract. After the ace of clubs, run six rounds of trumps, discarding two spades and two hearts *including the jack* from dummy, to give this position:

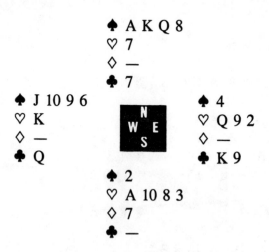

On the last trump West must either release the king of hearts or the queen of clubs. In the former case, declarer cashes the three spade winners and then finesses the ten of hearts for his contract. In the latter situation, the three top spades squeeze East in hearts and clubs. A sort of non-simultaneous guard double squeeze!

In the other room the French pair of Ghestem and Bacherich had an undistinguished auction. South opened 3♣, a transfer preempt showing diamonds, and in response to this North bid 4♠! Naturally it went all pass and France gained a rather lucky 11 IMPs.

Sometimes this entry-killing lead will break up a squeeze. You hold

♠ 7   ♡ J 8 6 3   ◊ Q 10 9   ♣ J 10 9 8 5

and hear the following auction:

West	North	East	South
	Pass	Pass	2♠ (a)
Pass	3♠	Pass	4♣
Pass	4NT (b)	Pass	5♣ (c)
Pass	7♠	Pass	Pass
Pass			

(a) Strong two-bid
(b) Roman Key Card Blackwood
(c) Three key cards

What is your opening lead?

At one table West tried a heart, whereas at the other the lead was a trump.

This was the full deal:

Dealer: North
Vulnerable: North-South

```
                    ♠ A 10 6 5
                    ♡ K 10 7 4
                    ◇ A 6 3
                    ♣ 7 3
    ♠ 7                             ♠ 2
    ♡ J 8 6 3         N             ♡ Q 5 2
    ◇ Q 10 9       W     E          ◇ J 7 4 2
    ♣ J 10 9 8 5      S             ♣ K Q 6 4 2
                    ♠ K Q J 9 8 4 3
                    ♡ A 9
                    ◇ K 8 5
                    ♣ A
```

The heart lead allowed the declarer to score three tricks in the suit and make his grand slam. The trump lead, though, forced declarer to work harder for his tricks. He won the lead and cashed four more rounds of spades, putting West under some pressure. He could not afford to discard a heart, so he chose to throw four clubs. Three rounds of hearts, declarer ruffing, and the ace of clubs left this situation:

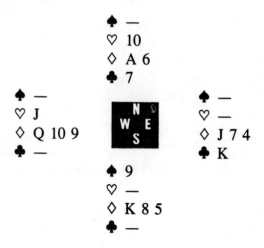

The last trump produced a classic double-squeeze position. And West could not have saved the day by retaining a club because of the guard-squeeze element in the diamond suit.

The killing lead is a diamond, which destroys declarer's communications.

e. The following example should be considered easy. Sitting West with both sides vulnerable, you hold

♠ K Q J 10   ♡ A 8 4 2   ◇ 9 3   ♣ 7 5 4

and participate in this competitive auction:

West	North	East	South
			1 ♡
1 ♠	2 ◇	2 ♠	3 ♣
Pass	3 ♡	Pass	4 ♡
Pass	Pass	Pass	

You might not approve of the 1 ♠ overcall, but it is not uncharacteristic of the matchpointed pairs game. It indicates a good lead to partner, and perhaps talks the opponents out of a makable 3 NT contract. However, this is not our concern here. This is a classic case for a forcing game. You have good trumps and a strong side suit, so you should plan to lead spades whenever possible and hope that declarer runs out of control.

This was the actual deal:

Dealer: South
Vulnerable: Both

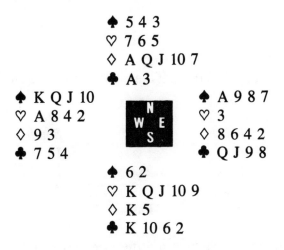

When declarer ruffs the third round of spades and leads trumps, you have to come to four tricks if you are careful to hold up your ace of hearts until the third round of the suit.

It is usually right to force declarer if you know he is in a poorish fit but has a second suit to fall back on as a source of tricks.

With neither side vulnerable, you are looking at

♠ 10 5 3   ♡ A Q 5 3 2   ◇ 9 5 4   ♣ K 8

The auction proceeds:

West	North	East	South
		1 ◇	1 ♠
Double (a)	Pass	2 ♡	3 ♣
3 ♡	3 ♠	Pass	4 ♠
Pass	Pass	Pass	

(a) Negative

What is your lead?

Would it make any difference if the bidding had been slightly different?

West	North	East	South
		1 ◇	Double
1 ♡	Pass	2 ♡	2 ♠
3 ♡	3 ♠	Pass	4 ♠
Pass	Pass	Pass	

On the actual deal was there a difference between the ace of hearts, which was the choice of the West who heard the first auction, and a trump, the selection of the West who took part in the second sequence?

This was the full deal:

Dealer: East
Vulnerable: None

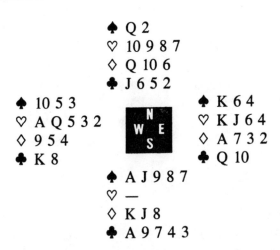

```
                    ♠ Q 2
                    ♡ 10 9 8 7
                    ◊ Q 10 6
                    ♣ J 6 5 2
   ♠ 10 5 3                      ♠ K 6 4
   ♡ A Q 5 3 2      N            ♡ K J 6 4
   ◊ 9 5 4       W     E         ◊ A 7 3 2
   ♣ K 8            S            ♣ Q 10
                    ♠ A J 9 8 7
                    ♡ —
                    ◊ K J 8
                    ♣ A 9 7 4 3
```

After the trump lead declarer was able to take advantage of the favorable breaks in both black suits and make 4♠ with an overtrick. But the declarer who was faced with the ace-of-hearts lead could not manage it; he had to lose the lead too often and was forced every time, in the end going two down.

Last in this section but most definitely not least, a beautiful but more difficult example from Hugh Kelsey's masterpiece, *Killing Defence at Bridge*. Once more you are West, and this time you are holding

♠ K 8 7 2   ♡ 5   ◇ A 7 6 3   ♣ K 9 6 4

You listen to the following auction:

West	North	East	South
			2♡ (a)
Pass	2NT (b)	Pass	3◇
Pass	3♠	Pass	4◇
Pass	4♡	Pass	Pass
Pass			

(a) Strong two-bid
(b) Negative response

What is your lead?

I trust you rejected the idea of leading your singleton trump; declarer probably does not need diamond ruffs in the dummy.

Do I hear a vote for a spade, trying to find partner with the queen? That is not the right lead: it is too dangerous, and even if partner does have the queen, it will probably not be sufficient to defeat the contract.

But suppose partner has four trumps, which is not unlikely, and that you can shorten declarer with forcing club leads. Now we are getting there. You assume partner has some strength in clubs and away you go! But wait a moment. If you have a good idea, do not act impulsively; consider the implications. If declarer is short in the suit, as you hope, you must start with the *king* of clubs, just in case the jack or queen is in the dummy and you need to pin a singleton honor in the South hand.

Look at the full diagram:

Dealer: South
Vulnerable: North-South

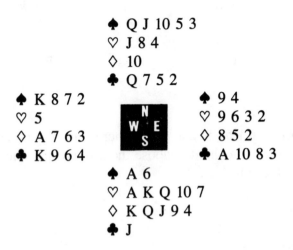

```
                    ♠ Q J 10 5 3
                    ♡ J 8 4
                    ◇ 10
                    ♣ Q 7 5 2
   ♠ K 8 7 2                        ♠ 9 4
   ♡ 5              N               ♡ 9 6 3 2
   ◇ A 7 6 3     W     E            ◇ 8 5 2
   ♣ K 9 6 4        S               ♣ A 10 8 3
                    ♠ A 6
                    ♡ A K Q 10 7
                    ◇ K Q J 9 4
                    ♣ J
```

Poor South! Once his Achilles' heel was found, he could not avoid his downfall. When he pitched his losing spade on the second round of clubs, West, who carefully followed the king with the nine, just continued with a third club to drive the final nail into the coffin.

(Not that it is relevant to this book, but I think North should have bid 4♡ over 3◇, not 3♠. He knows of at least an eight-card heart fit, and as his partner holds a two-suiter, he is unlikely to have spade support.)

To end this chapter, three interesting deals that do not really fit in elsewhere.

The first two make an interesting contrast.

With only your side vulnerable, you are the dealer holding

♠ Q 6   ♡ 10 3   ◇ 9 4 2   ♣ Q J 7 4 3 2

The auction proceeds:

West	North	East	South
Pass	Pass	2♠	3♡
Pass	3♠	Pass	5♡
Pass	6♡	Pass	Pass
Pass			

What is your lead?

In fact a trump lead is not so silly here, but if you decide to lead a spade, you should choose the six, not the queen.

This was the full deal:

Dealer: West
Vulnerable: East-West

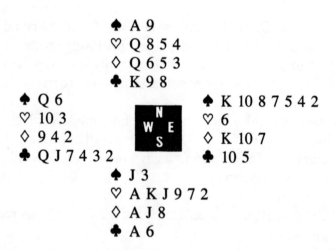

```
                    ♠ A 9
                    ♡ Q 8 5 4
                    ◇ Q 6 5 3
                    ♣ K 9 8
   ♠ Q 6                          ♠ K 10 8 7 5 4 2
   ♡ 10 3              N          ♡ 6
   ◇ 9 4 2          W   E         ◇ K 10 7
   ♣ Q J 7 4 3 2       S          ♣ 10 5
                    ♠ J 3
                    ♡ A K J 9 7 2
                    ◇ A J 8
                    ♣ A 6
```

At the table the queen of spades was led and declarer handled the play beautifully. He won with the ace and cashed six rounds of trumps to reach this position:

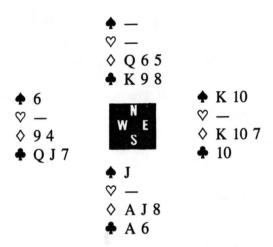

The ace and kings of clubs finished East. If he discarded a diamond, the whole suit would come in. Whereas if he threw the ten of spades, a diamond to the jack and a spade would endplay him to lead away from the king of diamonds. So he parted with the king of spades, hoping his partner had the jack, but that card became declarer's twelfth trick.

If only West still held the queen of spades in the above position!

This time the opponents are vulnerable and you are in fourth seat with

♠ K 10 5   ♡ 8 6   ◊ Q 9 3 2   ♣ Q 8 7 4

The bidding follows this path:

West	North	East	South
	1 ◊	1 ♠	2 ♡
Pass	4 ♡	Pass	4NT (a)
Pass	5 ♡	Pass	6 ♡
Pass	Pass	Pass	

(a) Ordinary Blackwood

What is your lead?

In fact I held this hand, playing in the flighted Swiss teams at the 1982 Mexican Nationals. It was clear partner had made a light overcall based on the vulnerability, and a spade lead seemed indicated, but I was worried that if I led a low one, I would be left with control of all three suits. So I selected the king of spades as my lead.

This proved to be the full deal:

Dealer: North
Vulnerable: North-South

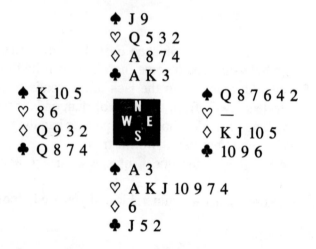

After my lead declarer could not make the contract. Whereas if I had led a low spade, dummy's nine would force partner's queen and allow declarer to endplay me with the king of spades to lead away from the queen of clubs after eliminating the diamonds.

Admittedly here, as in the previous hand, a trump lead (not to mention a diamond) would have defeated the slam, but if you are not going to open with a trump, it helps to know which card to choose from the holding in the suit you are going to lead.

Finally, perhaps the wildest deal in which I ever took part. It was a pairs event, both sides were vulnerable and sitting opposite me in the West chair was my wife, Edith, holding

♠ K 10 7 4   ♡ 8   ◊ Q 7 4   ♣ 9 8 6 3 2

The bidding proceeded:

West	North	East	South
			2♡ (a)
Pass	4♡	4NT (b)	5♡
Pass	Pass	6◊	Pass
Pass	6♡	7♣	Pass
Pass	7♡	Pass	Pass
Double	Pass	Pass	Pass

(a) Weak two-bid
(b) For the minors

What would you lead?

Obviously a club is less likely than a diamond to stand up and so Edith selected the queen of diamonds. This proved to be the winner when the full deal turned out to be:

Dealer: South
Vulnerable: Both

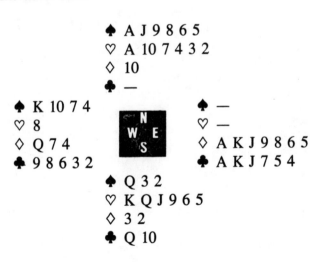

```
                ♠ A J 9 8 6 5
                ♡ A 10 7 4 3 2
                ◊ 10
                ♣ —
♠ K 10 7 4                        ♠ —
♡ 8              N                ♡ —
◊ Q 7 4       W     E             ◊ A K J 9 8 6 5
♣ 9 8 6 3 2      S                ♣ A K J 7 5 4
                ♠ Q 3 2
                ♡ K Q J 9 6 5
                ◊ 3 2
                ♣ Q 10
```

As you can see, 7♡ doubled makes on any other lead.

I had always intended to bid a grand slam on my cards, so I bid 6♦ before 7♣, rather than make another unusual-notrump bid, to show I had longer diamonds than clubs. And I did not double 7♡ just in case Edith thought I was making a Lightner double asking for a spade lead — which actually happened at one table.

That is a deal that would be difficult to follow, so this makes a good point at which to end the chapter and move on to considering when one should lead trumps.

Chapter 2

TO PROTECT HIGH CARD STRENGTH

Whither wilt thou lead me?

HAMLET, WILLIAM SHAKESPEARE

You are on lead against a suit contract. There are several factors that should be considered before you select the card you place on the table.

A. Review the bidding.

In fact it is a good idea to be doing this during the auction. Build up pictures of the opponents' hands (and your partner's, which is easier to do if he bids) as this will facilitate choosing the best lead.

B. Do you have an obvious lead?

Normally the clear-cut lead, if you have one, will be the most productive. But just because you are holding the ace-king-queen of a suit does not mean you should lead one of them without giving the matter a little more thought.

C. Eliminate the unattractive leads.

Go through the suits and mentally cross off the ones which you will definitely not lead.

D. Does a trump lead fall into one of the categories in the preceding chapter?

If it does, look for something else.

E. Are you still uncertain of what to lead?

If so, do not automatically dive for a trump.

F. Are you still thinking?

I hope so! One key reason why experts win at this game is that they put in more effort at the table than less-good players. The more you consider matters, the more likely you are to come up with the right answer.

By now you should have selected a lead — get on with the game and mentally keep your fingers crossed. (Ideally you should retain an even tempo in your play, but of course that is not always possible.)

At last it is time to consider trump leads. After some research and discussion with friends who are expert players, I have come up with 16 situations when a trump lead is likely to be best. Let us look at them in turn.

One of the most frequent and obvious reasons to lead a trump is the heading for this chapter: *To Protect High Card Strength.* This occurs most frequently in two types of auctions:

a. Partner has opened with a strong notrump or in some other way has indicated balanced strength

b. The opponents have taken a high-level sacrifice with few points, so must be relying on ruffs

In both of these situations you want to score as many of your high cards as possible by reducing the opponents' ruffing power.

With neither side vulnerable, you are sitting West and pick up

♠ Q 2   ♡ 9 7 6 5   ◇ 10 9 6 2   ♣ K 4 2

The bidding proceeds:

West	North	East	South
		1NT	2◇ (a)
Pass	Pass	Double	Pass
Pass	Pass		

(a) Pinpoint Astro showing diamonds and hearts

What do you lead?

Following principle *a*, I selected the two of diamonds. This was the complete deal:

Dealer: East
Vulnerable: None

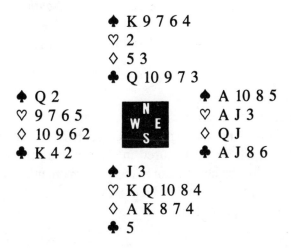

```
                    ♠ K 9 7 6 4
                    ♡ 2
                    ◊ 5 3
                    ♣ Q 10 9 7 3
    ♠ Q 2                              ♠ A 10 8 5
    ♡ 9 7 6 5          N               ♡ A J 3
    ◊ 10 9 6 2      W     E            ◊ Q J
    ♣ K 4 2            S               ♣ A J 8 6
                    ♠ J 3
                    ♡ K Q 10 8 4
                    ◊ A K 8 7 4
                    ♣ 5
```

Declarer won the first trick with the king of diamonds and played the king of hearts. My partner, Mauricio Smid, won with the ace and led back the queen of diamonds. Declarer won again, cashed the queen of hearts and then guessed correctly by leading a low heart to bring down the jack rather than trying to pin the nine with the ten. Now Smid made an excellent play: he underled his ace of clubs. I won with the king, cashed my two high trumps and exited with a club. Declarer took his heart winners but had to concede two spade tricks. That was two down and plus 300 gave us a great score.

It is also possible that you will wish to protect your own highcards when partner doubles the opponents.

With both sides vulnerable, you are the dealer holding

♠ J 10 9 7   ♡ A Q 6 3   ◇ A Q 10   ♣ Q 10

The bidding is:

West	North	East	South
1NT	2NT	Double	3♣
Pass	Pass	Double	Pass
Pass	Pass		

What is your opening lead?

Not difficult, is it, to appreciate the advantage of opening the queen of clubs? And that is precisely what Kirsten Møller, the wife of Steen whom we featured in the previous chapter, did when playing for the home team in the 1977 Women's European Championship in Elsinore, Denmark.

This was the complete deal:

Dealer: West
Vulnerable: Both

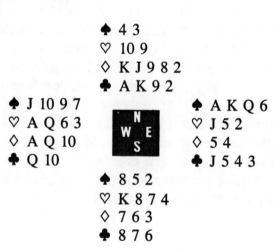

```
                ♠ 4 3
                ♡ 10 9
                ◇ K J 9 8 2
                ♣ A K 9 2
 ♠ J 10 9 7              ♠ A K Q 6
 ♡ A Q 6 3       N      ♡ J 5 2
 ◇ A Q 10     W   E     ◇ 5 4
 ♣ Q 10          S      ♣ J 5 4 3
                ♠ 8 5 2
                ♡ K 8 7 4
                ◇ 7 6 3
                ♣ 8 7 6
```

The first trick was won in the dummy, and the ten of hearts was run to West's queen. A second trump was won with dummy's king, and the nine of hearts went to the ace. Now West led the jack of spades, and continued with a second round to East's queen. Trine Hesselberg cashed the jack of clubs and exited with her last trump. This endplayed the dummy in diamonds. The declarer made only three trump tricks: a 1700-point lesson for North.

One other point: in neither of these cases was it likely that the trump lead would cost a trick in the suit. That is not necessarily the case on the next hand, but it is time to move on and consider situation *b*, when the opponents sacrifice against your contract.

It is unfavorable vulnerability, as it usually is when the opponents are sacrificing, and fourth-in-hand you hold

♠ K 10 5   ♡ K Q 9 8 7 4   ◇ K 5 4   ♣ 8

The bidding proceeds:

West	North	East	South
	Pass	1♠	2♣
2♡	3♣	3◇	4♣
4♠	5♣	Double	Pass
Pass	Pass		

What is your lead?

Yes, you guessed it: the eight of clubs, even though it is a singleton!

The complete layout was:

Dealer: North
Vulnerable: East-West

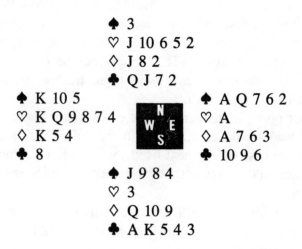

```
              ♠ 3
              ♡ J 10 6 5 2
              ◇ J 8 2
              ♣ Q J 7 2
♠ K 10 5                      ♠ A Q 7 6 2
♡ K Q 9 8 7 4                 ♡ A
◇ K 5 4                       ◇ A 7 6 3
♣ 8                           ♣ 10 9 6
              ♠ J 9 8 4
              ♡ 3
              ◇ Q 10 9
              ♣ A K 5 4 3
```

Declarer won the trump lead in the dummy and played a spade, but East went up with the ace and returned a second club. South could take one spade ruff, but he could not stop East regaining the lead to remove dummy's last trump. In all declarer lost three spades, one heart and two diamonds to finish four down: 700 to East-West.

Alternative leads allow the declarer to lose only 500, and with East-West making 4♠ in the other room, the lead made the difference between winning and losing points on the board.

The second example in this section comes from the 1973 Bermuda Bowl tournament in Guarujá, Brazil. It was board 23 of the final between Italy and the Aces. With both sides vulnerable, you are sitting West with

♠ 8 2   ♡ Q 7 4   ◇ A K 9 6 2   ♣ 9 4 3

The bidding proceeds:

West	North	East	South
Garozzo	*Wolff*	*Belladonna*	*Hamman*
			2♣ (a)
Pass	4♣ (b)	Double	5♣ (c)
Double	Pass	Pass	Pass

(a) Natural: a long club suit, perhaps a second suit and 12-16 points

(b) Preemptive

(c) Even more preemptive!

What is your lead?

It is getting easier. We all know you chose the three or four of clubs.

This was the full deal:

Dealer: South
Vulnerable: Both

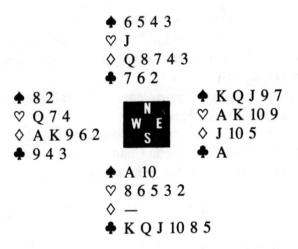

```
                    ♠ 6 5 4 3
                    ♡ J
                    ◊ Q 8 7 4 3
                    ♣ 7 6 2
    ♠ 8 2                          ♠ K Q J 9 7
    ♡ Q 7 4          N             ♡ A K 10 9
    ◊ A K 9 6 2    W   E           ◊ J 10 5
    ♣ 9 4 3          S             ♣ A
                    ♠ A 10
                    ♡ 8 6 5 3 2
                    ◊ —
                    ♣ K Q J 10 8 5
```

Note that if West leads a high diamond, declarer can escape for two down by ruffing hearts twice on the table. But Garozzo accurately led the three of clubs. East won with the ace and returned the king of spades, South ducking. On winning the spade continuation, declarer led a heart toward dummy.

The easy way to 800 now is for Garozzo to rise with the queen and play another trump. However, he went for a less pedestrian line by playing low so that Belladonna could win with the king and return a third round of spades. South ruffed high and Garozzo discarded a heart! Now Hamman could score only one ruff on the table, for on the third round of hearts West was able to ruff in with the nine of clubs and take out dummy's last trump. Thus South still lost five tricks: 800 to Italy.

This defense netted Italy 12 IMPs when the Americans were cautious in the other room:

West	North	East	South
Lawrence	Forquet	Goldman	Bianchi
			Pass
Pass	Pass	1 ♠	2 ♣
Pass	Pass	Double	Pass
2 ♠	Pass	Pass	Pass

West chose to underbid opposite his partner's double; but it is easier to say that he should bid more than to say exactly what he should bid. Also, no game is laydown, and in fact no game can make against double dummy defense.

My next example comes from another of Hugh Kelsey's excellent books: *101 Bridge Maxims*.

The hand occurred during the Ireland-Poland match in the Open Series of the 1967 European Championships in Dublin. With only your side vulnerable, you are West with

♠ A Q J 6   ♡ Q 4   ◇ J 4   ♣ J 10 9 7 6

The exciting auction goes:

West	North	East	South
Klukowski	*Shrage*	*Wajrodzki*	*Read*
			Pass
1♣	Pass	1♦	1♠
Pass	Pass	3♣ (a)	4♡
Pass	Pass	4NT	5♣
Double	5♡	Pass	Pass
Double	Pass	6♣	Pass
Pass	6♡	Double	Pass
Pass	Pass		

(a) Forcing

I am sorry I cannot supply more information about the bidding; but despite that handicap, what is your lead?

At the time West led the jack of diamonds, which produced a disappointing result for his side when the full deal proved to be:

Dealer: South
Vulnerable: East-West

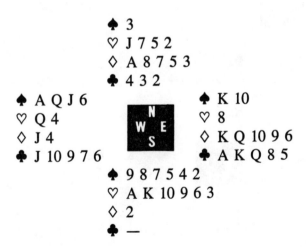

```
                    ♠ 3
                    ♡ J 7 5 2
                    ◇ A 8 7 5 3
                    ♣ 4 3 2
  ♠ A Q J 6                        ♠ K 10
  ♡ Q 4              N             ♡ 8
  ◇ J 4            W   E           ◇ K Q 10 9 6
  ♣ J 10 9 7 6       S             ♣ A K Q 8 5
                    ♠ 9 8 7 5 4 2
                    ♡ A K 10 9 6 3
                    ◇ 2
                    ♣ —
```

Dummy won the first trick with the ace of diamonds, a spade was won with East's ten, the club switch ruffed, the ace of hearts cashed, the spade suit set up with three ruffs in the dummy and 1210 written on the scoresheet. Not bad to make a slam with only 12 high card points between the two hands!

With all three suits clearly held, West should have led the four of hearts. The best declarer can do then is to win in hand and lead a low spade, putting West to the test. As the cards lie, he must go up with an honor in order to be able to play a second round of trumps.

In the other room the Poles were doubled in 5 ♡ and made the same 12 tricks after a non-trump lead. That gave Poland 750, but Ireland gained 10 IMPs whereas they could have lost 13 if West had defeated the slam.

Kelsey's maxim for this hand is that if you have strength in three suits yet the opponents outbid you in the fourth, they must have distributional values and so you should lead a trump to cut down their ruffs.

It can also be right to lead a trump when partner is marked with strength in three suits. This example makes an interesting defensive problem.

Dealer: South
Vulnerable: None

```
              ♠ J 6 4
              ♡ Q 10 8 4 3
              ◊ A 8 4 2
              ♣ 6
                          ♠ 5
                          ♡ K J 7 2
                          ◊ K Q 7 5
                          ♣ Q J 9 2
```

West	North	East	South
			1 ♠
Pass	2 ♠	Double	4 ♠
Double	Pass	Pass	Pass

Your partner leads the nine of spades. Declarer wins in hand and runs the nine of diamonds to your queen, partner contributing the three. What do you lead now?

You want to get partner on lead again so that he can play a second round of trumps. Does he have the ace of hearts or ace of clubs?

At the table it looked very dangerous to East to play a heart with the queen-ten sitting on the dummy, so he led a club. That let the contract make when the full deal proved to be:

Dealer: South
Vulnerable: None

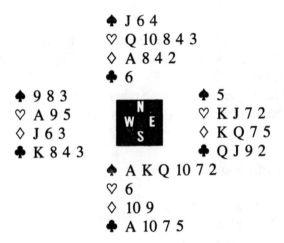

♠ J 6 4
♡ Q 10 8 4 3
♢ A 8 4 2
♣ 6

♠ 9 8 3
♡ A 9 5
♢ J 6 3
♣ K 8 4 3

♠ 5
♡ K J 7 2
♢ K Q 7 5
♣ Q J 9 2

♠ A K Q 10 7 2
♡ 6
♢ 10 9
♣ A 10 7 5

Declarer calmly cross-ruffed to ten tricks on the club return.

Should East have been able to find the winning play? Yes, for the reason explained by West at the time. His double of 4♠ must have indicated two key cards. These were either the ace-king of clubs or the ace of hearts and a club honor. If he held the former, West would surely have led one of them, not a trump. So it was correct to play West for the ace of hearts. As you can see, a heart to West's ace and a second round of trumps reduces declarer's tricks to nine.

On the next deal there is a change: the opponents are

vulnerable and you are not. As always, though, you are West, holding

♠ Q   ♡ K J 10   ◇ K J 7 6 4   ♣ A K Q 5

And once more the bidding is exciting:

West	North	East	South
			1♠
Double	2♣	Pass	Pass
Double	Pass	2NT	3♡
Double	3♣	Pass	Pass
Double	Pass	Pass	Pass

When did you last make just four doubles in an auction? Anyway, I think I know what you will be leading: the queen of spades, *n'est-ce pas?*

As you will have guessed, because otherwise the hand would not be in this book, that is the killing lead, the full deal being:

Dealer: South
Vulnerable: North-South

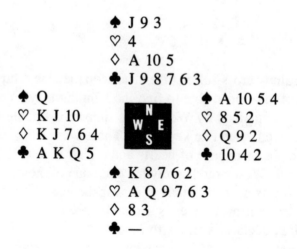

```
                    ♠ J 9 3
                    ♡ 4
                    ◇ A 10 5
                    ♣ J 9 8 7 6 3
   ♠ Q                              ♠ A 10 5 4
   ♡ K J 10          N              ♡ 8 5 2
   ◇ K J 7 6 4     W   E            ◇ Q 9 2
   ♣ A K Q 5         S              ♣ 10 4 2
                    ♠ K 8 7 6 2
                    ♡ A Q 9 7 6 3
                    ◇ 8 3
                    ♣ —
```

East does best to win your lead with the ace and return a second trump, netting 500 for your side. However, even if he ducks, declarer will go one down.

At the time, though, West led a top club in order to have a look at the dummy. It proved fatal when declarer was able to ruff, cash the ace of hearts and cross-ruff hearts and clubs to reach this position with the lead in the South hand:

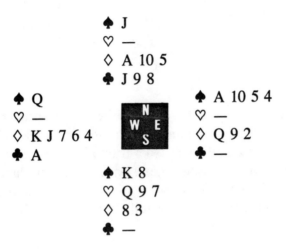

Declarer played a winning heart and the defenders could not stop him making three more tricks.

If West had ruffed with the queen of spades and played a diamond, declarer would have won with the ace and led a club, so West chose to discard a diamond. Dummy ruffed with the jack of spades and East was forced to overruff with the ace. A trump went to South's king, but a diamond to the ace and a club let declarer score his eight of spades with a *coup en passant*.

Even if West throws his ace of clubs, East overruffs with the ace of spades and switches to a diamond, declarer has a counter: he just ducks the first round of diamonds.

For my final example in this chapter, another relatively common situation in which a trump lead is usually best — you hold strength in declarer's second suit.

With neither side vulnerable, you hold

♠ 10 8 7 6   ♥ Q J 10   ♦ 8 3   ♣ A Q 10 8

The opponents have the following uncontested auction:

West	North	East	South
			1 ♠
Pass	2 ♠	Pass	3 ♣ (a)
Pass	4 ♠	Pass	Pass
Pass			

(a) Long-suit game-try

It is likely that dummy is short in clubs because he probably does not have a fitting club honor. Also, you are unlikely to cost your side a trick in the suit, so a trump lead seems best.

That was how Mike Passell, one of America's best players and a winner of the Bermuda Bowl in 1979, reasoned, and his analysis was vindicated when the full deal proved to be:

Dealer: South
Vulnerable: None

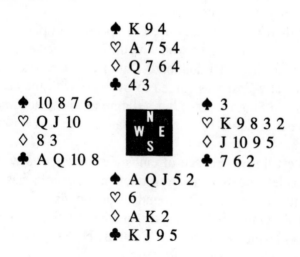

♠ K 9 4
♥ A 7 5 4
♦ Q 7 6 4
♣ 4 3

♠ 10 8 7 6   ♠ 3
♥ Q J 10   ♥ K 9 8 3 2
♦ 8 3   ♦ J 10 9 5
♣ A Q 10 8   ♣ 7 6 2

♠ A Q J 5 2
♥ 6
♦ A K 2
♣ K J 9 5

When dummy appeared declarer saw that all he needed was a club trick or a club ruff in the dummy for his tenth trick. In an effort to obtain either, he led twice toward his club holding, but on both occasions Passell won the trick and played another trump. After that, declarer had to hope that either the diamonds were breaking or the ace of clubs was now a singleton, but his luck was out and he went one down. Without the trump lead it is not difficult to engineer the club ruff. And declarer can also handle heart forces.

One word of warning here, however. If you judge that both pairs are fitting in two suits, it will probably be wrong to lead a trump. There will be a risk that the opponents will not be needing ruffs, and that you should cash the tricks in your suits first.

Chapter 3

TO CUT DOWN THE OPPONENTS' RUFFING POTENTIAL

Oh, Amos Cottle! — Phoebus! what a name
To fill the speaking trump of future fame!

ENGLISH BARDS AND SCOTCH REVIEWERS, LORD BYRON

Next to protecting high card strength, the main purpose of an opening trump lead is to stop the opposition from scoring ruffs in either hand. Of course, this can hardly be accomplished completely, but to hold the declarer to a minimum number of ruffs will often pay rich dividends, and here are some of the situations in which it will usually pay to lead a trump.

An Opponent has a Three-Suiter

As usual, the best indicator for this action is the bidding. Whenever an opponent has advertised a three-suiter (or partial three-suiter), a trump lead is highly desirable.

Some conventional opening bids announce three-suiters: 2♣ in the Roman Club system, 2♢ in both Precision Club and Roman, and Flannery (which will be considered a partial three-suiter for our purposes).

Here are some examples of the efficacy of a trump lead after one of these opening bids. The first comes from the 1953 Bermuda Bowl match in New York between Sweden and the United States.

Sitting West, you hold

♠ J 7 4 2   ♡ Q 9   ♢ K 9 4   ♣ J 9 8 3

and you hear the opponents run the following auction:

West	North	East	South
Becker	Larsen	Crawford	Wohlin
	2♣ (a)	Pass	2♦ (b)
Pass	3♣ (c)	Pass	3♡
Pass	Pass	Pass	

(a) A weak three-suiter
(b) Asking for the singleton
(c) Singleton club

And your lead?

The queen of hearts, of course! The complete deal was as follows:

Dealer: North
Vulnerable: East-West

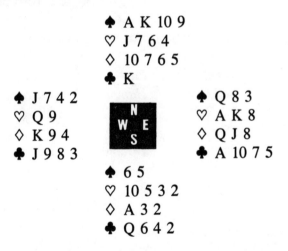

```
                    ♠ A K 10 9
                    ♡ J 7 6 4
                    ◊ 10 7 6 5
                    ♣ K
    ♠ J 7 4 2                        ♠ Q 8 3
    ♡ Q 9              N             ♡ A K 8
    ◊ K 9 4       W        E         ◊ Q J 8
    ♣ J 9 8 3         S             ♣ A 10 7 5
                    ♠ 6 5
                    ♡ 10 5 3 2
                    ◊ A 3 2
                    ♣ Q 6 4 2
```

B. J. Becker led the queen of hearts and continued trumps. East, John Crawford, took the king and ace before switching to the ace and another club, leaving the declarer, Jan Wohlin, two down even though he was able to take two spade finesses.

This was the supposedly natural auction in the other room:

73

West	North	East	South
Lilliehöök	Rapée	Anulf	Schenken
	Pass	1 ♣	Pass
1 ◊	Double	Redouble	1 ♡
1 ♠	2 ♡	Pass	Pass
Pass			

Nils-Olof Lilliehöök led the three of clubs and East, Gunnar Anulf, upon winning with the ace, made the unfortunate continuation of the ace, king and another heart, felling his partner's queen in the process. By finessing twice in spades, George Rapée was able to make eight tricks, giving the U.S. a gain of 210 points (IMP scoring was not in use in those days).

The next example comes from round 14 of the round robin section of the 1973 Bermuda Bowl tournament. You are sitting in Bobby Wolff's chair with

♠ J 8 7 6   ♡ 8 2   ◊ K Q   ♣ K J 10 6 5

and the Italian Precision auction proceeds as follows:

West	North	East	South
Wolff	Belladonna	Hamman	Garozzo
	2 ◊ (a)	Pass	2 ♡ (b)
Pass	3 ♡ (c)	Pass	4 ♡ (d)
Pass	Pass	Double	Pass
Pass	Pass		

(a) Three-suiter, short in diamonds
(b) In principle, to play
(c) Invitational
(d) Always ready to gamble!

What is your opening lead?

Don't tell me — you lead a trump, right? Not a bad choice as the full deal proved to be:

Dealer: North
Vulnerable: East-West

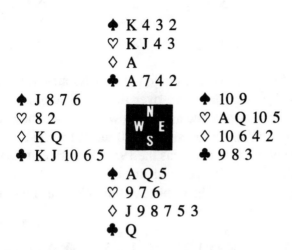

```
                 ♠ K 4 3 2
                 ♡ K J 4 3
                 ◊ A
                 ♣ A 7 4 2
  ♠ J 8 7 6                      ♠ 10 9
  ♡ 8 2              N           ♡ A Q 10 5
  ◊ K Q          W     E         ◊ 10 6 4 2
  ♣ K J 10 6 5      S            ♣ 9 8 3
                 ♠ A Q 5
                 ♡ 9 7 6
                 ◊ J 9 8 7 5 3
                 ♣ Q
```

As the World Championship book states, a trump lead is marked even without the double. Wolff duly led the two of hearts, Hamman won the trick with the ten and returned a diamond to the ace. Garozzo took in order the ace of spades, a diamond ruff, the queen of spades, the ace of clubs and a club ruff before leading the jack of diamonds. Wolff ruffed with the eight of hearts, and dummy overruffed with the jack. Declarer had seven tricks at this point, and could have made two more by continuing the minor-suit cross-ruff, but he unwisely attempted to cash the king of spades first and made no more tricks. Hamman carefully ruffed with the queen of hearts, guarding against the possibility that declarer was now void in spades, cashed the ace of hearts and played a club for his partner to take two tricks in the suit.

That gave the American pair a 500 penalty. The auction in the other room was:

West	North	East	South
Forquet	*Goldman*	*Bianchi*	*Lawrence*
	1♣	Pass	1◊
Pass	1NT	Pass	2◊
Pass	Pass	Pass	

Goldman knew his partner could not have a four-card major unless he had enough to move over the 1 NT rebid.

2 ◊ came home when declarer led low on the second round of trumps, giving the Aces another 90 and 11 IMPs.

The scene of the next deal was the 1980 World Team Olympiad in Valkenburg. It occurred during the match between Australia and Norway. Once more sitting West, at favorable vulnerability, you hold

♠ A 5   ♡ K Q J 9   ◊ J 8 5   ♣ A Q 9 4

and you take part in this auction:

West	North	East	South
Nordby	*Lavings*	*Aabye*	*Klinger*
	Pass	Pass	2♡ (a)
Double (b)	Pass	Pass (c)	Pass

(a) Either Flannery with four spades and five hearts or 4-4-4-1 shape and a minor-suit singleton
(b) A strong balanced hand
(c) Converting to penalties

What is your lead?

There should be no question in your mind: the king of hearts. Let us look at the complete deal:

Dealer: North
Vulnerable: North-South

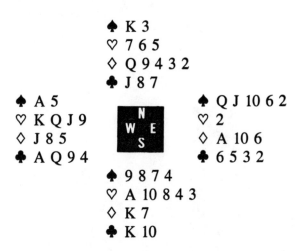

```
                    ♠ K 3
                    ♡ 7 6 5
                    ◊ Q 9 4 3 2
                    ♣ J 8 7
    ♠ A 5                        ♠ Q J 10 6 2
    ♡ K Q J 9          N         ♡ 2
    ◊ J 8 5         W     E      ◊ A 10 6
    ♣ A Q 9 4          S         ♣ 6 5 3 2
                    ♠ 9 8 7 4
                    ♡ A 10 8 4 3
                    ◊ K 7
                    ♣ K 10
```

Harald Nordby led the king of hearts, which was allowed to hold, and continued with the jack, which Ron Klinger won with the ace. When declarer played a spade toward the king, West went in with the ace and exited in the same suit. A diamond to the king was followed by a spade, and Nordby ruffed with the nine of hearts, cashed the queen to draw dummy's last trump and played a diamond. This allowed the defenders to take four more tricks (one diamond, one spade and two clubs) and register 800 in the plus column.

The play is rather more complicated in the next deal. It comes from the United States-Israel match in the 1976 World Team Olympiad in Monte Carlo; and shows a relatively frequent situation of a partial three-suiter being easily recognized as opener bids out his shape. And by way of variety, I will set it as a play problem against a you-know-what lead:

Dealer: South
Vulnerable: None

♠ K Q 8
♡ 8 7
◇ A K 8
♣ A K 7 6 3

♠ A J 10 5
♡ 10 9 6
◇ Q 10 3 2
♣ 9 5

The auction was identical at both tables:

West	North	East	South
Lev	Hamilton	Romik	Eisenberg
Soloway	Shaufel	Rubin	Frydrich
			Pass
Pass	1♣	Pass	1♠
Pass	2◇	Pass	3◇
Pass	3♠	Pass	4♠
Pass	Pass		

It is one of those irritating hands where 3 NT is fine if the defense cannot or does not take five heart tricks, but both Souths were expecting North to have a singleton heart and so went for the Moysian 4-3 fit.

A trump was led at both tables, without which it would have been easy for the declarers to organize a heart ruff in the dummy for their tenth trick. However, after the trump lead there are several possible lines of play, some of which work and some of which do not. What is your choice?

Billy Eisenberg won the opening lead in the dummy and opted to play off three rounds of diamonds. When Pinhas Romik ruffed the third and played a second trump, declarer stood no chance. He tried for a 3-3 club break, but it was not to be.

Julian Frydrich went for what appears to be a better line. He won the trump lead in the dummy and attacked the clubs immediately, discarding a heart from hand on the third round of the suit. The defenders took their two heart tricks before playing a second trump. Declarer cashed the ace-king of diamonds to see if the jack was dropping, and when it did not he ruffed a club high and relied on a 3-3 spade break, making his contract and gaining 10 IMPs for Israel.

The full deal was:

Dealer: South
Vulnerable: None

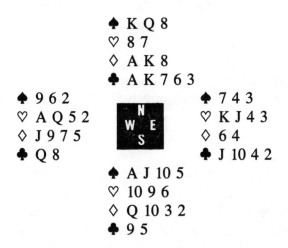

```
              ♠ K Q 8
              ♡ 8 7
              ◊ A K 8
              ♣ A K 7 6 3
  ♠ 9 6 2                    ♠ 7 4 3
  ♡ A Q 5 2          N       ♡ K J 4 3
  ◊ J 9 7 5       W     E    ◊ 6 4
  ♣ Q 8              S       ♣ J 10 4 2
              ♠ A J 10 5
              ♡ 10 9 6
              ◊ Q 10 3 2
              ♣ 9 5
```

The best line of play, pointed out to me by Eddie Wold, was missed at both tables. You should win the first trick in the dummy and then *duck* a club. This retains all the options.

Assuming they play a second round of spades, you draw all the trumps. When they break 3-3, you set up the clubs. However, if the spades are 4-2, you try first for a 3-3 club break, and if that fails to materialize, you hope the diamond suit will produce four tricks.

Note also that in this case the trump lead did not automatically defeat four spades, but it was the only one to give the defenders a chance at a plus score.

One last example in this section. You are playing against a pair using the Blue Club system, both sides are vulnerable, and you are holding

♠ J   ♡ K 8 6   ◊ A K 9 7 5   ♣ J 9 6 5

The bidding proceeds:

West	North	East	South
			2 ◊ (a)
Pass	2 ♡ (b)	Pass	3 ♣ (c)
Pass	3 ◊ (b)	Pass	3 ♠ (d)
Pass	4 ♠	Pass	Pass
Pass			

(a) Any 4-4-4-1 shape and 17-24 points
(b) A relay asking for further definition
(c) 4-4-1-4 shape (singleton diamond) and 17-20 points
(d) 19 or 20 points

What is your opening lead?

Sitting West during an Italian championship in 1970 was one of the world's most talented players, Arturo Franco. Despite the fact that he held a singleton, Franco knew that a trump lead would be best as declarer had announced a three-suiter. Therefore he placed the jack of spades on the table.

This was what he could see:

Dealer: South
Vulnerable: Both

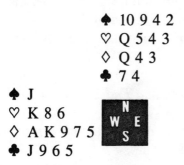

```
                    ♠ 10 9 4 2
                    ♡ Q 5 4 3
                    ◊ Q 4 3
                    ♣ 7 4
♠ J
♡ K 8 6
◊ A K 9 7 5
♣ J 9 6 5
```

Declarer won the first trick with the queen of spades and led his singleton jack of diamonds. How would you defend?

I found this deal in *Focus on Bridge Defence,* an excellent book written by the renowned Danish author, Aksel Nielsen.

Franco realized that desperate measures were needed to stand any chance of defeating the game, so he won the second trick with the king of diamonds and switched to the six of hearts.

This was the full deal:

Dealer: South
Vulnerable: Both

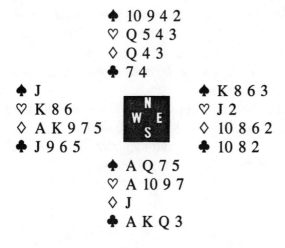

```
                    ♠ 10 9 4 2
                    ♡ Q 5 4 3
                    ◊ Q 4 3
                    ♣ 7 4
♠ J                                  ♠ K 8 6 3
♡ K 8 6                              ♡ J 2
◊ A K 9 7 5                          ◊ 10 8 6 2
♣ J 9 6 5                            ♣ 10 8 2
                    ♠ A Q 7 5
                    ♡ A 10 9 7
                    ◊ J
                    ♣ A K Q 3
```

Unable to believe that Franco would lead away from the king in this position, declarer played low from the dummy, and East's jack forced the ace. Not fatal, but South was dead after his next play: the ace of spades. The third round of trumps was taken by East's king, a heart went to the king and a heart ruff defeated the game.

The Opponents bid Three Suits and End Up in a Fourth

In this situation it is dollars to doughnuts that a trump lead is best, even when it is a singleton.

At unfavorable vulnerability, you are sitting West and holding

♠ 2   ♡ K 10 9 8   ◊ J 10 9 4   ♣ Q 7 5 2

The bidding proceeds:

West	North	East	South
	1 ♣	Pass	1 ◊
Pass	1 ♡	Pass	1 ♠
Pass	2 ♠	Pass	4 ♠
Pass	Pass	Pass	

What is your opening lead?

While you are pondering, an observation about the above sequence. It is not the standard expert practice, but a good way to play is that South's 1 ♠ rebid shows four spades and is forcing, whereas if South rebids 2 ♠ instead, that is fourth suit forcing and denies four spades.

Both red suits look unattractive, so perhaps at the table last week, before reading this book, you would have led a club. Now, of course, you start with your singleton spade and defeat the contract when the full deal turns out to be:

Dealer: North
Vulnerable: East-West

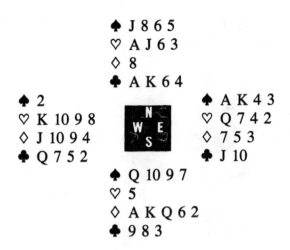

♠ J 8 6 5
♥ A J 6 3
♦ 8
♣ A K 6 4

♠ 2
♥ K 10 9 8
♦ J 10 9 4
♣ Q 7 5 2

♠ A K 4 3
♥ Q 7 4 2
♦ 7 5 3
♣ J 10

♠ Q 10 9 7
♥ 5
♦ A K Q 6 2
♣ 9 8 3

Along the same lines, a hand from the 1978 Mexican Mixed Pairs Championship when my wife, Edith, was my partner. Sitting West, you hold

♠ K 6 3   ♥ 6 5 3   ♦ K J 9 2   ♣ Q J 3

and, as above, the bidding proceeds:

West	North	East	South
	1♣	Pass	1♦
Pass	1♥	Pass	1♠
Pass	2♠	Pass	4♠
Pass	Pass	Pass	

You lead a trump, of course, and this turns out to be the complete deal:

Dealer: North
Vulnerable: North-South

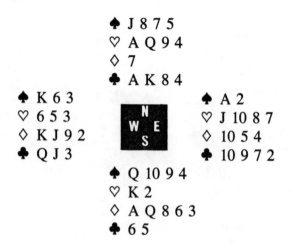

♠ J 8 7 5
♡ A Q 9 4
♢ 7
♣ A K 8 4

♠ K 6 3
♡ 6 5 3
♢ K J 9 2
♣ Q J 3

♠ A 2
♡ J 10 8 7
♢ 10 5 4
♣ 10 9 7 2

♠ Q 10 9 4
♡ K 2
♢ A Q 8 6 3
♣ 6 5

I won the first trick with the ace of spades, returned the suit and Edith played a third round, on which I had to discard the four of diamonds.

We had reduced declarer's trump tricks to three, so he tried an elimination and endplay. He cashed the ace-king of clubs, under which Edith carefully unblocked the queen and jack, and ruffed the third round. Next came three top hearts, followed by the seven of diamonds. Declarer was hoping to ride that, but I covered with the ten to force him into finessing the queen and condemning him to one down.

The Opponents find a Fit, Dabble at Notrump but End up in the Suit

If the opponents locate a fit, one of them then suggests notrump instead but partner returns to the suit, it indicates that that hand has a shortage and a trump lead will probably be effective.

Here is an example from the 1980 Mexican Open Pairs. The uncontested auction was a simple 1♠ - 2♠ / 3 NT - 4♠ / Pass and the player on lead held

♠ 9 7 3   ♡ A Q 6   ◊ 8 5 4   ♣ K 10 7 2

Eddie Wold had no hesitation in advancing the seven of
spades, the middle card from three-low in our methods.
This was the full deal:

Dealer: South
Vulnerable:

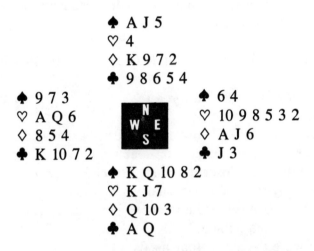

        ♠ A J 5
        ♡ 4
        ◊ K 9 7 2
        ♣ 9 8 6 5 4

♠ 9 7 3   ♠ 6 4
♡ A Q 6   ♡ 10 9 8 5 3 2
◊ 8 5 4   ◊ A J 6
♣ K 10 7 2   ♣ J 3

        ♠ K Q 10 8 2
        ♡ K J 7
        ◊ Q 10 3
        ♣ A Q

After the trump lead declarer decided to abandon any hope
of heart ruffs in the dummy and went after the diamond suit
instead. He guessed correctly by winning the first trick in dummy and playing a diamond to the ten. He continued with the
queen, which I ducked, and a third round to my ace. I returned
the ten of hearts and when declarer covered with the jack, Wold
won with the queen and played a second spade.

Now declarer could either draw the last trump and cash the
thirteenth diamond, or take a heart ruff in the dummy. He made
the logical decision to do the former and rely on the club finesse,
but it lost and he was one down.

Notice that if declarer does not cover my ten of hearts, I

switch to a club; and that 3 NT makes if declarer guesses correctly in diamonds — or in both red suits if West is inspired enough to lead the queen of hearts.

The Declarer has bid Two Suits and Received Preference for the Second

If you have declarer's first suit well held behind him, you should lead a trump. But what if you are short in declarer's first suit?

Here is an interesting example from the 1983 National Open Pairs. Sitting West, you hold

♠ J 9   ♡ 8 3   ◇ A K Q 2   ♣ 10 7 6 4 2

and hear the opponents bid 1 ♠ - 1 NT / 2 ♡ - Pass. What do you lead?

It is a difficult choice between a trump and a diamond honor. If the declarer has a singleton or doubleton diamond, he may be able to discard a loser if dummy has club strength, which is not unlikely. On the other hand, partner may have natural tricks in the spade suit and it might be imperative to cut down spade ruffs in the dummy.

These were the actual four hands:

Dealer: South
Vulnerable: East-West

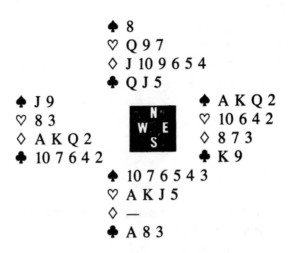

```
                  ♠ 8
                  ♡ Q 9 7
                  ◇ J 10 9 6 5 4
                  ♣ Q J 5
   ♠ J 9                         ♠ A K Q 2
   ♡ 8 3                         ♡ 10 6 4 2
   ◇ A K Q 2                     ◇ 8 7 3
   ♣ 10 7 6 4 2                  ♣ K 9
                  ♠ 10 7 6 5 4 3
                  ♡ A K J 5
                  ◇ —
                  ♣ A 8 3
```

As this event was a matchpointed pairs, Eddie Wold decided to lead a diamond honor for the reasons described above. Unfortunately, declarer was able to ruff it and immediately play a low spade. Wold won and switched to a trump, but it was too late. Declarer came to eight tricks via two spade ruffs, three hearts, one diamond ruff and two clubs.

In this particular case it takes a trump lead to defeat 2♡. Wold commented afterwards that he probably would have led one at teams with IMP scoring, but at pairs he did not want to go against the field and risk a bottom.

Dummy is Unbalanced with only Three-Card Trump Support

Sometimes you can tell from the bidding that this is the situation, and it may be important to lead a trump to cut down the number of possible ruffs in the dummy.

Here is an example from the 1969 Trials match between the Aces and a California quartet. You are West, the dealer at unfavorable vulnerability, and your hand is

♠ 9 8 5 3   ♡ K 7 5   ◊ A 5   ♣ A J 8 5

The bidding proceeds:

West	North	East	South
Swanson	Wolff	Walsh	Jacoby
1♣	2◊ (a)	Pass	2♡
Pass	3♡	Pass	4♡
Pass	Pass	Pass	

(a) Weak

What is your lead?

No doubt you chose a trump and gave declarer no chance when the full deal proved to be:

Dealer: West
Vulnerable: East-West

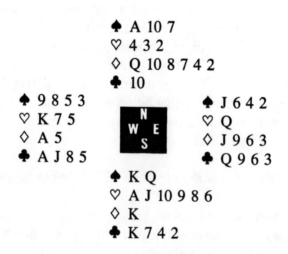

```
                    ♠ A 10 7
                    ♡ 4 3 2
                    ◊ Q 10 8 7 4 2
                    ♣ 10
    ♠ 9 8 5 3                        ♠ J 6 4 2
    ♡ K 7 5          N               ♡ Q
    ◊ A 5          W   E             ◊ J 9 6 3
    ♣ A J 8 5         S              ♣ Q 9 6 3
                    ♠ K Q
                    ♡ A J 10 9 8 6
                    ◊ K
                    ♣ K 7 4 2
```

At the time, though, John Swanson led the nine of spades, which ran to the king. With the actual lie of the cards, Jim Jacoby could have guaranteed his contract now by leading a low club from hand, but he played the king of diamonds. This gave West a second chance to lead the fatal trump, but Swanson won with the ace and persevered with spades. Now it is all over: Jacoby won with the queen, led a club, won the queen-of-hearts return, ruffed a club, discarded his last two clubs on the ace of spades and queen of diamonds and conceded a trump.

In the other room the auction was:

West	North	East	South
Eisenberg	Hallee	Goldman	Soloway
1♣	2♦	Pass	Pass
Pass			

This made exactly and the Aces gained eight IMPs. They proceeded to win the match and, the following year, the world championship: America's first Bermuda Bowl victory in 16 years.

Finally in this section, hand 98 from the 1955 Bermuda Bowl, England's only victory in this event.

The opponents are vulnerable and you are the dealer holding:

♠ J 7 5   ♡ 6 5 2   ♦ Q 5   ♣ K Q J 5 3

An ordinary-looking collection, but the bidding is far from ordinary:

West	North	East	South
Ellenby	Reese	Rosen	Schapiro
Pass	1♣	1♠	2♡
2♠	3♡	4♠	5♡
Pass	Pass	Double	Pass
Pass	Redouble	Pass	Pass
Pass			

What is your lead?

I suppose I should have sneaked in a deal where a trump lead would have been a disaster, but not this time! Milton Ellenby led the king of clubs and regretted his decision when the full deal proved to be:

Dealer: West
Vulnerable: North-South

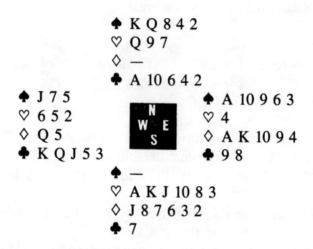

```
                    ♠ K Q 8 4 2
                    ♡ Q 9 7
                    ◇ —
                    ♣ A 10 6 4 2
    ♠ J 7 5                         ♠ A 10 9 6 3
    ♡ 6 5 2              N          ♡ 4
    ◇ Q 5            W       E      ◇ A K 10 9 4
    ♣ K Q J 5 3         S          ♣ 9 8
                    ♠ —
                    ♡ A K J 10 8 3
                    ◇ J 8 7 6 3 2
                    ♣ 7
```

When North redoubles it is obvious that he would be happy to hear the opponents run to 5♠, so he must have length and strength in that suit. Along with his clubs, this means he is probably short in diamonds. And even if East has a club void, he must have a lot of diamonds, in which case a trump could still be the killing lead.

Boris Schapiro won the king-of-clubs lead with the ace, played the king of spades and ruffed out the ace, trumped a diamond in the dummy, discarded a diamond on the queen of spades and proceeded to cross-ruff clubs and diamonds until dummy's trumps were exhausted. This left declarer with two diamond losers but his redoubled contract with 100 honors, which still counted in those days: 1250 to England.

In the Closed Room the bidding was almost as exciting:

West	North	East	South
Konstam	Moran	Meredith	Mathe
Pass	1♣	1♠	2♡
Pass	3♡	3♠	4♠
Pass	5♣	Pass	5♡
Pass	Pass	Pass	

Kenneth Konstam also led the king of clubs. The play was effectively the same, so the United States scored 750 points but lost 500 on the board.

If only Ellenby had led a trump, the U.S. would have gained 300 (don't forget those honors!) in the Open Room — a total difference of 1550. Not enough to reverse the result of the match, but it would have made a psychological difference with another 126 boards to go.

Dummy has Four-Card Support, but a Cross-Ruff is Likely

Even if you know that dummy is coming down with four-card support, it could still be right to lead a trump if you feel declarer is proposing to make the majority of his tricks by way of a cross-ruff.

The first example arose during the final quarter of one of my team's matches in the 1981 Vanderbilt.

You are sitting in the chair of Eric Rodwell, neither side is vulnerable and your hand is

♠ Q 10 6   ♡ 7 4   ◇ K 5 4 3   ♣ J 9 7 2

The bidding proceeds:

West	North	East	South
			1♡
Pass	4♢ (a)	Pass	4NT (b)
Pass	5♡ (c)	Pass	6♡
Pass	Pass	Pass	

(a) Splinter bid
(b) Roman Key Card Blackwood
(c) Two key cards but no queen of hearts

What is your lead?

Often against a slam that has been bid in a confident-sounding fashion you should make an aggressive lead, but here Rodwell could not be sure that either black suit was going to be the winner, and he appreciated the likelihood of a cross-ruff as dummy was coming down with a singleton diamond. So he led the four of hearts; and this proved to be the full deal:

Dealer: South
Vulnerable: None

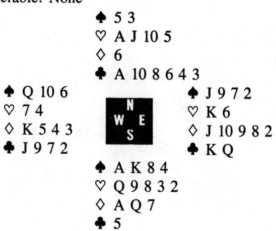

North was Gail Moss (now Greenberg) and South was Jacqui Mitchell, and they had bid an excellent slam with only 24 high card points between the two hands. The slam was almost certain to make if either the trump finesse won or the clubs were breaking 3-3. And with the prevailing distribution declarer could have succeeded against a black-suit lead, making the tricks on a cross-ruff if East never ruffs in with the king of hearts or setting up the clubs and running them if he does. However, after the actual trump lead declarer had no chance. She finessed at trick one, East, Jeff Meckstroth, won with the king and returned a second trump. Declarer started on the clubs, but when they turned out to be 4-2, she was forced to endplay West with the last club to force a diamond lead into the ace-queen to escape for one down.

In the other room we were happy with game and so gained a lucky 11 IMPs. As we won the match by only eight points, if the slam had made, we would have lost by 14; and if Mitchell and Moss had stopped in game, we would have lost by three — assuming all the other results had been the same.

On the second example of this section, both sides are vulnerable and you hold

♠ K J 6   ♡ A K J   ◊ 7 4 3 2   ♣ J 6 3

The bidding goes:

West	North	East	South
	1 ◊	Pass	1 ♠
Pass	1NT	Pass	2 ♡
Pass	3 ♡	Pass	4 ♡
Pass	Pass	Pass	

What is your opening lead?

You know that the opponents do not have the normal high-card values for this contract as 2 ♡ could have ended the auction. In this situation it is usually right to lead a trump, so let us assume you start with the ace or king. This is what you can see after the dummy comes down:

Dealer: North
Vulnerable: Both

```
                    ♠ 5
                    ♡ 9 8 7 2
                    ◇ A Q 7 6
                    ♣ A K Q 7
    ♠ K J 6              N
    ♡ A K J          W       E
    ◇ 7 4 3 2            S
    ♣ J 6 3
```

Partner plays the six of hearts at the first trick; how do you continue?

Did you switch to diamonds or continue with your trumps, potentially sacrificing a trick in the suit?

You should realize that a diamond play will serve no purpose as declarer will be able to discard any losers in the suit on dummy's club winners. This is the time for playing trumps.

This was the full deal:

Dealer: North
Vulnerable: Both

```
                    ♠ 5
                    ♡ 9 8 7 2
                    ◇ A Q 6 5
                    ♣ A K Q 7
    ♠ K J 6              N          ♠ Q 10 8 3
    ♡ A K J          W       E      ♡ 6
    ◇ 7 4 3 2            S          ◇ K J 9
    ♣ J 6 3                         ♣ 10 9 8 5 2
                    ♠ A 9 7 4 2
                    ♡ Q 10 5 4 3
                    ◇ 10 8
                    ♣ 4
```

After three rounds of trumps, declarer must guess the diamond position to make ten tricks. He must play to ruff out the king rather than rely on the finesse.

After the actual club lead, declarer took dummy's three club winners, throwing a diamond and a spade, and then cross-ruffed in spades and diamonds. West just made three trump tricks.

As was the case in these two hands, one usually knows from the bidding when this sort of situation exists and that a trump lead is required.

You are Long in Trumps

When the opponents come to rest in a suit in which you have considerable length, you probably feel that your luck has finally taken a turn for the better. But it is not a time to be complacent. It could well be best for you to lead a trump. If your holding does not contain any honors, perhaps you will be cutting down the amount of cross-ruffing declarer will be able to do. And if you have a lot of honors, even if you sacrifice a trick initially, it might well come back. And in this latter situation, there is a risk you will be endplayed to lead away from your holding if you cannot reduce your length in time.

Here are two examples. In the first you hold

♠ 6 5 4 3 2   ♡ 7 4   ◇ A 7 3   ♣ J 9 8

The opponents are vulnerable, and the auction goes:

West	North	East	South
			1♣
Pass	1◊	2♡ (a)	Pass
Pass	3♡	Pass	3♠
Pass	4NT (b)	Pass	5♠ (c)
Pass	6♠	Pass	Pass
Pass			

(a) Weak

(b) Roman Key Card Blackwood

(c) Two of the five key cards and the queen of spades

At the table, West led a heart, but that allowed the slam to make as the full deal was:

Dealer: South
Vulnerable: North-South

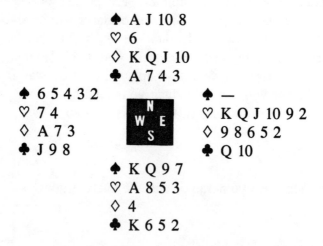

♠ A J 10 8
♡ 6
◊ K Q J 10
♣ A 7 4 3

♠ 6 5 4 3 2
♡ 7 4
◊ A 7 3
♣ J 9 8

♠ —
♡ K Q J 10 9 2
◊ 9 8 6 5 2
♣ Q 10

♠ K Q 9 7
♡ A 8 5 3
◊ 4
♣ K 6 5 2

Declarer won the heart lead with the ace, ruffed a heart in the dummy and led the king of diamonds. West won with the ace and switched to a trump, but it was too late. Declarer won in the dummy, discarded two clubs on the queen-jack of diamonds, cashed the ace-king of clubs and cross-ruffed the rest of the tricks, West being forced to underruff four times.

If only West had led a trump and continued a second round when in with the ace of diamonds, declarer could not have made his contract.

Once more the vulnerability is favorable, and playing in a pairs event sitting West, you hold

♠ K J 10 9 8   ♡ K 9 5   ◊ J 8 6   ♣ 5 3

South, the dealer, opens 1♠, and it is passed round to your partner, who doubles. As it is a pairs, you decide to try for the magic plus 200 by passing. What is your opening lead?

At the time, everyone led a heart, but as you will have guessed, a trump lead is the only winner (and the king is the correct card in case dummy or partner has a singleton queen.) This was the full deal:

Dealer: South
Vulnerable: North-South

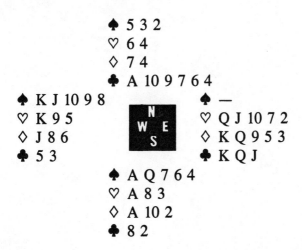

```
                    ♠ 5 3 2
                    ♡ 6 4
                    ◊ 7 4
                    ♣ A 10 9 7 6 4
    ♠ K J 10 9 8              ♠ —
    ♡ K 9 5          N        ♡ Q J 10 7 2
    ◊ J 8 6       W     E     ◊ K Q 9 5 3
    ♣ 5 3            S        ♣ K Q J
                    ♠ A Q 7 6 4
                    ♡ A 8 3
                    ◊ A 10 2
                    ♣ 8 2
```

Declarer ducked the actual lead, won, say, the heart continuation, ducked a diamond, won the club switch, played a diamond to the ace, ruffed a diamond, crossed to the ace of hearts, ruffed a heart and cast adrift with a club. Eventually

West had to ruff in and lead into declarer's ace-queen of spades. It was strange to see so many plus 160s on the travelling scoreslip.

However, if West had led the king of spades, the defense could have triumphed. West can gain the lead in both red suits, once to drive out the queen of spades and once to draw trumps, with the result that declarer obtains only one ruff in the dummy and finishes one down.

This just goes to show how impossible it is to do the right thing every time at the bridge table!

Chapter 4

CLUES FROM DOUBLES

Double, double toil and trouble;
Fire burn, and cauldron bubble.

MACBETH, WILLIAM SHAKESPEARE

Partner Passes Your Take-Out Double

One of the first things a beginner learns is that if partner passes his one-level take-out double, converting it to a penalty double, he must *always* lead a trump. One can hardly quarrel with such a sound and simple rule except maybe for the use of the categorical "always." Like every bridge writer, I have learned by experience to avoid words like "never" and "always."

Here is an example illustrating this principle. It occurred at the 1980 World Team Olympiad in the match between Egypt and Israel, that historic first sporting encounter between the two countries.

Sitting West with both sides vulnerable, you hold

♠ A J 9 5   ♡ J 7   ◇ K 10   ♣ A Q J 10 7

You take part in the following short but spicy auction:

West	North	East	South
Birman	Abdel Kadar	Frydrich	Makram
		Pass	1 ♡ (a)
Double	Pass	Pass	Pass

(a) Maybe only a four-card major.

What do you lead?

No doubt the jack of hearts was on the table before I had asked you!

This was the full deal:

Dealer: East
Vulnerable: Both

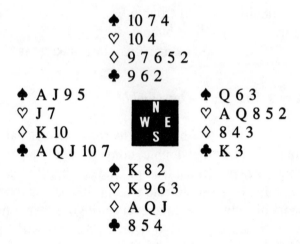

```
              ♠ 10 7 4
              ♡ 10 4
              ◊ 9 7 6 5 2
              ♣ 9 6 2
♠ A J 9 5                    ♠ Q 6 3
♡ J 7            N           ♡ A Q 8 5 2
◊ K 10        W   E          ◊ 8 4 3
♣ A Q J 10 7     S           ♣ K 3
              ♠ K 8 2
              ♡ K 9 6 3
              ◊ A Q J
              ♣ 8 5 4
```

The declarer should not have passed out 1 ♡ doubled. East had told him that was the wrong contract for his side, so he should have made an SOS redouble, being willing to play in partner's longest suit. However, Sameh Makram was unlucky to pay such a high price.

He won the first trick with the king of hearts and led a low club. David Birman put in the ten so that he could play his second trump, won with the queen. Julian Frydrich cashed the king of clubs before switching to a low spade. West won with the jack, played off the ace of clubs, upon which East threw a spade, and followed with the ace and another spade for Frydrich to ruff. A diamond through declarer, the finesse losing, and a diamond back allowed Makram to cash a second diamond trick, but then at trick 12 he had to lead away from

100

his nine-six of hearts into East's ace-eight tenace. Four down and 1100 to Israel.

Egypt had a chance to obtain a penalty in the other room, but it was not easy for them to take it.

West	North	East	South
Sadek	Schwarz	Khalil	Stampf
		Pass	1NT (a)
Double	2 ◇	3 ♡	Pass
4 ♡	Pass	Pass	Pass

(a) 12-14 points

2 ◇ doubled probably would have cost 800, but it is never easy to double at a low level when you do not have much in the trump suit. Here some expert partnerships might have managed it because East would have made a forcing pass over 2 ◇, and West would have doubled in the protective seat to *suggest,* rather than insist on, penalties as he was sitting under the length. With his balanced hand, East would not be averse to defending.

As it was, Samih Khalil lost only one diamond and two heart tricks to make 4 ♡; but Israel gained 10 IMPs.

Following a Penalty Double of a Partscore Contract

Most experts extend the principle of trump leads to include all low-level partscore contracts. Benito Garozzo once said: "When I double a partscore I want my partner to lead a trump; he has no other choice!"

The following deal from the 1973 Bermuda Bowl round robin match between Italy and the Aces lends weight to his views; and suggests that he should follow his own dictum!

Sitting West at favorable vulnerability, Garozzo held

♠ 2   ♡ A J 10 6 4 2   ◇ Q 5 3   ♣ A 9 7

The bidding went:

West	North	East	South
Garozzo	*Wolff*	*Belladonna*	*Hamman*
		1 ◊ (a)	1 ♠
2 ♡	2 ♠	Double	Pass
Pass	Pass		

(a) Precision

What would you lead?

After the preamble, you will have selected the two of spades, of course; but Garozzo chose the three of diamonds. That was not ideal when the full hand proved to be:

Dealer: East
Vulnerable: North-South

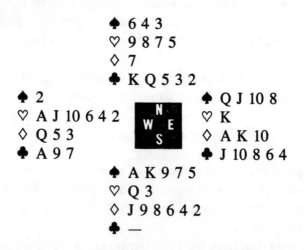

Giorgio Belladonna's 1 ◊ opener was correct in the Precision system: his suit was not good enough for two clubs.

East won the first trick with the king of diamonds, cashed the king of hearts and returned the queen of spades. Bob Hamman won with the ace, ruffed a diamond and ran the king of clubs, discarding the queen of hearts. Garozzo won with the ace and returned a club, declarer discarding a diamond. That left this position:

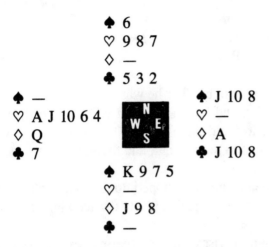

```
              ♠ 6
              ♡ 9 8 7
              ◇ —
              ♣ 5 3 2
♠ —                          ♠ J 10 8
♡ A J 10 6 4      N          ♡ —
◇ Q            W   E         ◇ A
♣ 7               S          ♣ J 10 8
              ♠ K 9 7 5
              ♡ —
              ◇ J 9 8
              ♣ —
```

Declarer ruffed a heart, on which East threw the ace of diamonds, and trumped a diamond in the dummy. Belladonna was able to overruff, but it did him no good because it was with a natural trump trick and left declarer with greater spade length. Hamman ruffed the club exit, cashed the king of spades and reverted to diamonds. East could ruff whenever he liked, but South had the rest: 670 to the Aces.

There are two ways to defeat the contract. The more difficult is after the actual lead. East has to switch to the queen of spades at trick two without first cashing the king of hearts. And when West wins a trick with the ace of clubs, he must underlead the ace of hearts to his partner's king so that a second round of trumps can be led.

The easier method is for West to lead a trump at trick one! This was the auction in the other room:

West	North	East	South
Goldman	*Forquet*	*Lawrence*	*Bianchi*
		1♣	1♠
2♡	2♠	Double	3♢
3♡	Pass	3NT	Pass
Pass	Pass		

When Benito Bianchi bid 3 ♢ he was putting himself in 800 territory if doubled and left there. And if Pietro Forquet did go back to 3♠, it could have cost 500. But it was not easy for Bobby Goldman to realize that, and the Americans reached 3 NT.

When the queen of hearts dropped doubleton, declarer was able to make eleven tricks, losing just to the ace-king of spades, and giving the Aces 15 IMPs.

A similar situation arises when partner passes your negative double following an overcall of his opening bid.

This example arose in a club duplicate in Mexico. Sitting West once more, you hold

♠ 5 3   ♡ A K 10 7   ♢ K J 8 5 4 2   ♣ 5

and hear the auction proceed:

West	North	East	South
		1♠	2♣
Double (a)	Pass	Pass	Pass

(a) Negative, in principle showing length in the unbid suits

What is your lead?

This is a close decision because partner rates to be short in hearts, making a top heart an attractive proposition. The five of spades or a low diamond are also possible; but one of my Romex teammates, Sol Dubson, found the killing start when he led the five of clubs. The four hands were:

Dealer: East
Vulnerable: None

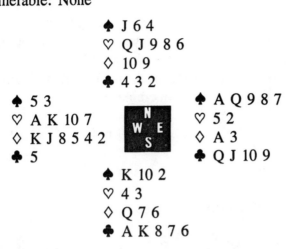

```
              ♠ J 6 4
              ♡ Q J 9 8 6
              ◇ 10 9
              ♣ 4 3 2
   ♠ 5 3                    ♠ A Q 9 8 7
   ♡ A K 10 7       N       ♡ 5 2
   ◇ K J 8 5 4 2  W   E     ◇ A 3
   ♣ 5               S      ♣ Q J 10 9
              ♠ K 10 2
              ♡ 4 3
              ◇ Q 7 6
              ♣ A K 8 7 6
```

Declarer won the trump lead with the ace and immediately attacked diamonds in an attempt to score a ruff in the dummy. East won the first round with the ace and played a second trump to declarer's king. The second diamond was taken with West's jack and a spade switch went to the ace. East took his two trump winners and exited with a heart. West cashed the king and ace before reverting to diamonds, leaving declarer endplayed in his hand to lead away from the king-ten of spades. Thus South made only three trump tricks and the king of spades — four down!

An initial heart lead followed by a trump switch at trick two is equally effective, but a spade or diamond lead would prematurely remove one of East's entries, allowing declarer to engineer an extra trick. If East overruffs a diamond, declarer makes an additional trump trick.

An Opponent Pulls his Partner's Penalty Double

Occasionally it is an opponent's double which provides one with a helpful hint. This may occur when one of the enemy has not passed after his partner has made a penalty double. Such action is usually based on a distributional hand and the best way to keep his ruffs to a minimum is with an immediate trump lead. Of course, the player who removes his partner's double may think that the penalty inflicted will not compensate adequately for the game or slam makable by his side.

The following deal appeared in Alan Truscott's column.

As West, with both sides vulnerable, you hold

♠ 7 4 3   ♡ K 8 2   ◇ 10 9 6 4   ♣ A 10 5

The bidding goes:

West	North	East	South
		1♡	1♠
2♡	3♠	4♡	Double
Pass	4♠	Pass	Pass
Pass			

What is your lead?

The complete layout was:

Dealer: East
Vulnerable: Both

```
                    ♠ Q J 6 2
                    ♡ —
                    ◇ K 8 5 2
                    ♣ 8 7 6 4 3
        ♠ 7 4 3                    ♠ 9
        ♡ K 8 2         N          ♡ A J 9 7 4 3
        ◇ 10 9 6 4   W     E       ◇ Q J
        ♣ A 10 5        S          ♣ K Q 9 2
                    ♠ A K 10 8 5
                    ♡ Q 10 6 5
                    ◇ A 7 3
                    ♣ J
```

In contrast to the previous example, an initial trump lead is the only one that will defeat the contract. On any other start declarer scores three heart ruffs, two diamonds and five trumps in hand. However, if a trump is led, declarer lacks sufficient entries to his hand for three heart ruffs. When a club is played from dummy, West wins with the ace, if necessary overtaking his partner's honor, and persists with a second trump, limiting declarer to two heart ruffs and only nine tricks.

Partner Refuses to Balance Despite Known Strength

As in the Sherlock Holmes story about the dog that did not bark, the opening leader can draw useful inferences from his partner's failure to balance with a double or an overcall when he is marked with high-card strength.

This is a typical situation, taken from the 1981 Grand Nationals.

The bidding, with North-South vulnerable, went:

West	North	East	South
			1 ♣
Pass	Pass	Pass	

What do you lead from this hand?

    ♠ J 9 7 4   ♡ Q 10 6 5   ◇ K 6 5   ♣ 8 7

Partner is marked with high cards; why didn't he double or reopen with a suit or notrump bid? As you are relatively short in clubs, he probably has length in the suit and is afraid of pushing the opponents to a better spot. Therefore, you should lead a trump.

A look at the four hands confirms this diagnosis.

Dealer: South
Vulnerable: North-South

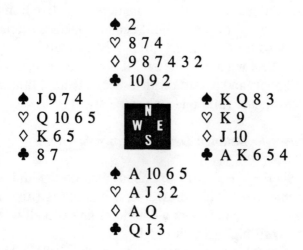

```
                    ♠ 2
                    ♡ 8 7 4
                    ◊ 9 8 7 4 3 2
                    ♣ 10 9 2
    ♠ J 9 7 4                    ♠ K Q 8 3
    ♡ Q 10 6 5          N        ♡ K 9
    ◊ K 6 5         W       E    ◊ J 10
    ♣ 8 7               S        ♣ A K 6 5 4
                    ♠ A 10 6 5
                    ♡ A J 3 2
                    ◊ A Q
                    ♣ Q J 3
```

The trump lead held declarer to four tricks: three aces and a trump. A heart lead permits declarer to score two additional spade ruffs in the dummy, going only one down (unless he risks the diamond finesse in an attempt to make his contract). On a spade lead, declarer can achieve three ruffs in the dummy and fulfill his contract. Finally, after a diamond lead declarer will make an overtrick. What a difference a lead makes!

Chapter 5

DECEPTIVE TRUMP LEADS

O what a tangled web we weave,
When first we practise to deceive!

MARION, SIR WALTER SCOTT

Ask a group of experts for their preference between a brilliant technical play and a successful deceptive move and I predict the latter will receive an overwhelming vote in the poll. Nothing fills the heart of a bridge player with more joy than bringing off a deceptive coup. Is this to be interpreted as the triumph of artful psychology over cold technical competence? Who knows; but as Plato wrote: "Everything that deceives may be said to enchant."

There are opportunities for deceptive trump leads from a variety of holdings, but they all have one principle in common: they create or increase the probability of declarer's choosing an option which was less attractive before the lead was made.

Here is an example which occurred in a tournament in Copenhagen. As West I held

♠ A 8 6   ♡ J 10 9   ◊ K 10 9 4 2   ♣ Q 6

and the bidding, with neither side vulnerable, proceeded:

West	North	East	South
	1 ♣	Pass	1 ♡
Pass	1 ♠	Pass	2NT
Pass	3 ♡	Pass	4 ♡
Pass	Pass	Pass	

As no lead seemed attractive, I decided on a trump and opted for a deceptive ten of hearts. After all, I should practice what I preach!

This was the complete layout:

Dealer: North
Vulnerable: None

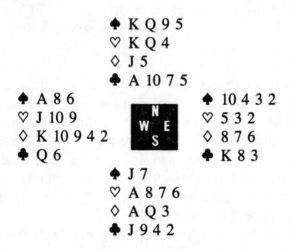

♠ K Q 9 5
♡ K Q 4
◇ J 5
♣ A 10 7 5

♠ A 8 6
♡ J 10 9
◇ K 10 9 4 2
♣ Q 6

♠ 10 4 3 2
♡ 5 3 2
◇ 8 7 6
♣ K 8 3

♠ J 7
♡ A 8 7 6
◇ A Q 3
♣ J 9 4 2

Of course, declarer would have been better off in the safe 3 NT game, and probably both players should have bid it on the third round of the auction.

However, in 4♡ declarer had a loser in every side suit as the diamond finesse was not working. So he had to bring in the trump suit without loss, and who can blame him for the line he adopted? After winning trick one in the dummy, he led a low spade to the jack and my ace. I persisted with the nine of hearts, following my original plan. After winning with dummy's queen, declarer tried the losing diamond finesse and I exited with the eight of spades. South led the four of hearts from the dummy and, after a suspicious look in my direction, finessed the eight, losing to my jack. Shaking his head, he murmured sadly, "I should have known . . ."

Soon after the article featuring this hand appeared in the

A.C.B.L. *Bulletin,* one of the players at our local club in Mexico City led the ten from jack-ten-nine and sadly Edith fell for it, finessing on the third round and losing to the jack. At which point the opening leader turned to me and said "I didn't know how many people read your articles, but *I* do!"

Another attractive holding which lends itself under certain circumstances to a deceptive trump lead is a doubleton honor: 10x, Jx, Qx or Kx.

The 1976 World Team Olympiad in Monte Carlo produced such an example, and it was discussed by Hugh Kelsey and John Matheson in their instructive book, *Improve Your Opening Leads.*

With both sides vulnerable, West held

♠ 10 6 5 2   ♡ J 9   ◇ 8 3   ♣ 7 6 5 3 2

and heard the auction proceed:

West	North	East	South
			1♣ (a)
Pass	1NT (b)	Pass	2♡ (c)
Pass	2♠ (d)	Pass	2NT (e)
Pass	4♡ (f)	Pass	6♡
Pass	Pass	Pass	

(a) Precision; 16+ HCPs
(b) Balanced 8-13 points
(c) Natural and asking
(d) Denies a heart holding as good as queen-third and denies four controls (A=2; K=1)
(e) Waiting, normally with no second suit
(f) Four low hearts

What do you lead?

The bidding tells you that the opponents have a nine-card heart holding and two relatively balanced hands. The side-suit leads are fraught with danger as you may finesse partner's holding and save declarer a guess. In contrast, a trump lead is likely to be safe as partner cannot hold more than two cards in the suit. You cannot give away a trick — on the contrary, if partner has the doubleton queen or king, you create a losing option for declarer which did not exist before.

These were the four hands:

Dealer: South
Vulnerable: Both

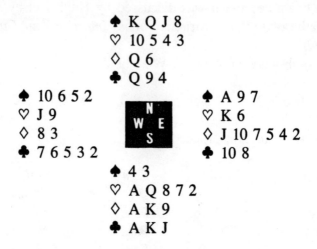

```
                    ♠ K Q J 8
                    ♡ 10 5 4 3
                    ◊ Q 6
                    ♣ Q 9 4
    ♠ 10 6 5 2                      ♠ A 9 7
    ♡ J 9              N            ♡ K 6
    ◊ 8 3          W     E         ◊ J 10 7 5 4 2
    ♣ 7 6 5 3 2       S            ♣ 10 8
                    ♠ 4 3
                    ♡ A Q 8 7 2
                    ◊ A K 9
                    ♣ A K J
```

The slam was bid 23 times and failed only once. At the table where the 'winning' lead was found, the bidding was not as informative as that given above. In fact it went

South	West	North	East
2♣	Pass	2♠	Pass
3♡	Pass	4♡	Pass
4NT	Pass	5♣	Pass
5◊	Pass	6♡	Pass
Pass	Pass		

That makes it all the more impressive that Benito Garozzo found the lead of the nine of hearts. Dummy covered with the ten,

East, Arturo Franco, played the king and declarer won with the ace. A diamond to the queen was followed by a finesse of the eight of hearts, losing to the jack. The ace of spades defeated the slam and Italy gained 17 IMPs when 6♡ was made in the other room.

Of course, it is easy to be wise after the event, saying it is unlikely Garozzo would lead a singleton trump, but he specializes in the unpredictable, especially when it sounds as though the contract is likely to make.

The next example comes from John Brown's timeless classic, *Winning Defence*. You are on lead against a contract of 4♡ holding

♠ A J 6 4 2   ♡ 10 9   ◊ J 9   ♣ A J 7 4

The bidding has proceeded:

West	North	East	South
			1♡
1♠	2◊	2♠	Pass
Pass	3♡	Pass	4♡
Pass	Pass	Pass	

What do you lead?
    This was the full deal:

Dealer: South
Vulnerable: Both

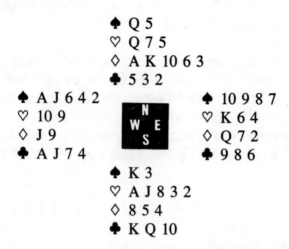

```
                    ♠ Q 5
                    ♡ Q 7 5
                    ◇ A K 10 6 3
                    ♣ 5 3 2
     ♠ A J 6 4 2                    ♠ 10 9 8 7
     ♡ 10 9          N             ♡ K 6 4
     ◇ J 9        W     E          ◇ Q 7 2
     ♣ A J 7 4       S             ♣ 9 8 6
                    ♠ K 3
                    ♡ A J 8 3 2
                    ◇ 8 5 4
                    ♣ K Q 10
```

The lead of ace and another spade leaves declarer being forced to guess the trump suit correctly. He will probably unblock the king of spades at trick one, and then lead a heart to the jack at trick three. When the nine appears on his left, he has to decide whether the suit is distributed like this:

> *Dummy*
> ♡ Q 7 5
>
> *West*   *East*
> ♡ 10 9   ♡ K 6 4
>
> *Declarer*
> ♡ A J 8 3 2

or thus:

> *Dummy*
> ♡ Q 7 5
>
> *West*   *East*
> ♡ 10 9 6   ♡ K 4
>
> *Declarer*
> ♡ A J 8 3 2

114

Note that the false card of the nine is mandatory in the second case in order to give declarer a losing option: a deceptive trump play rather than lead; and that therefore one cannot apply the Principle of Restricted Choice.

Against a strong player sitting West, declarer would have a guess. But as Brown pointed out, declarer can be given a gentle nudge in the wrong direction if West leads the nine of hearts at trick one. Expecting this to be West's top card in the suit, declarer will probably put up dummy's queen and capture the king with the ace. A diamond to the dummy and a finesse of the eight of hearts will leave the contract one down.

Once more, it is easy with hindsight to regard the nine of hearts lead with suspicion as the textbooks recommend the lead of the six from nine-six doubleton, but in the heat of the moment this sort of play usually works. (And next time you hold nine doubleton, think about leading the nine rather than the lower card.)

This layout is similar to the above.

```
                    Dummy
                    J 4 2
        West                    East
        10 9 5                  K 3
                    Declarer
                    A Q 8 7 6
```

Left to his own devices, declarer will finesse the queen and follow with the ace unless West drops the nine or ten under the queen, giving declarer the losing option of trying to pin the ten-nine doubleton.

But suppose West leads the nine at trick one. Declarer might feel East is looking at the K105 or K103 and put up the jack at trick one, planning a later finesse of the eight.

Here is another lead problem on this theme. With both sides vulnerable, you hold

♠ 9 2   ♡ K 7 6 4   ◇ A Q J 4   ♣ K J 6

The auction is slightly unusual:

West	North	East	South
1 ◇	4 ◇	5 ◇	5 ♠
Double	Pass	Pass	Pass

North's 4 ◇ overcall shows a four-spade preempt with little or no defensive values, whereas 4 ♠ would have guaranteed some cards outside the suit. It would seem more sensible to play these two bids the other way round, but that is not our concern here.

What is your lead?

Did you try the nine of spades? If so, you fell for the ruse in my introduction! This was the full deal:

Dealer: West
Vulnerable: Both

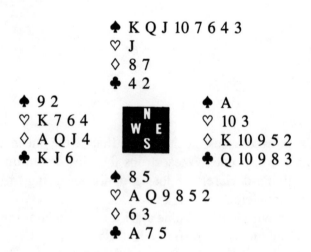

```
                    ♠ K Q J 10 7 6 4 3
                    ♡ J
                    ◇ 8 7
                    ♣ 4 2
    ♠ 9 2                              ♠ A
    ♡ K 7 6 4          N              ♡ 10 3
    ◇ A Q J 4       W     E           ◇ K 10 9 5 2
    ♣ K J 6            S              ♣ Q 10 9 8 3
                    ♠ 8 5
                    ♡ A Q 9 8 5 2
                    ◇ 6 3
                    ♣ A 7 5
```

At the table West, trying to reduce ruffs in the South hand, did lead the nine of spades and regretted his decision when his partner won with the ace and tried a club through rather than

116

a diamond. Declarer won with the ace, cashed the ace of hearts and played the queen, pinning the ten in the process. After ruffing out the king, he was able to return to hand with a spade to the eight and make an overtrick. If only West had led his low spade! (Perhaps the ace of diamonds is the most sensible lead, though a club also works.)

The following is a risky lead, but if you find the right situation, it will probably succeed:

                    Dummy
                    7 6 4 3
West   *East*
Q 2   J 8
                    Declarer
                    A K 10 9 5

A low trump is led away from the queen doubleton! Declarer will win the jack with the king and, concluding East is looking at QJ8, is likely to finesse the ten on the second round, losing to the queen.

Once more an option has been created by the lead that was not previously available to the declarer. He is left wondering whether or not to try to benefit from a situation that will not exist at other tables, at the same time risking suffering the embarrassment of losing to an opponent who came bearing a Greek gift.

Alan Truscott drew my attention to the following hand that occurred during the 1982 Olympiad in Biarritz. Sitting in the West seat was Ahsan Abbasi from Kuwait. He was looking at

♠ K J 7 2   ♡ Q 10   ◇ 10 7 6 3   ♣ 8 7 4

and the auction proceeded as follows:

West	North	East	South
			1NT (a)
Pass	2◇ (b)	Pass	2♡
Pass	3◇	Pass	3♠
Double	Pass	Pass	4♣
Pass	4◇	Pass	4♡
Pass	5♡	Pass	6♡
Pass	Pass	Pass	

(a) 15-17 high card points
(b) Transfer

What would you lead?
  This was the full deal:

Dealer: South
Vulnerable: None

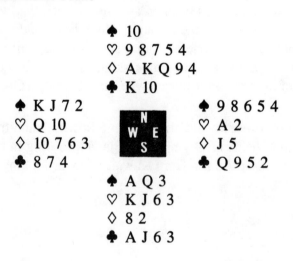

```
                    ♠ 10
                    ♡ 9 8 7 5 4
                    ◇ A K Q 9 4
                    ♣ K 10
  ♠ K J 7 2                        ♠ 9 8 6 5 4
  ♡ Q 10            N              ♡ A 2
  ◇ 10 7 6 3      W   E            ◇ J 5
  ♣ 8 7 4           S              ♣ Q 9 5 2
                    ♠ A Q 3
                    ♡ K J 6 3
                    ◇ 8 2
                    ♣ A J 6 3
```

Abbasi led the ten of hearts! His partner won with the ace and switched to a spade. Declarer was completely taken in. He

118

won with the ace of spades, crossed to the king of clubs and led a trump. When East followed with the two, declarer added salt to his own wounds by making a claim, stating that he would finesse the jack of hearts, cash the king and have 12 tricks. He was surprised and disappointed to hear this courteous demurrer from his left:

"I'd be pleased to concede your claim, however, the laws require me to follow suit and I cannot help taking this trick with the queen. But the rest indeed are yours."

Both sides are vulnerable, and you are surveying

♠ Q J 10   ♡ K 8 5 2   ◇ 9 8 4 3   ♣ Q 2

The bidding proceeds:

West	North	East	South
			1 ♣
Pass	1 ◇	Pass	1 ♡
Pass	3 ♣ (a)	Pass	3NT
Pass	4 ♣	Pass	4 ♡
Pass	4 ♠	Pass	5 ♠
Pass	6 ♣	Pass	Pass
Pass			

(a) Forcing

What is your lead?

Playing in The Golfers' Club in Paris in 1966, Cino del Duca, after whom the marvelous tournament held every June in the French capital is named, felt desperate measures were needed, and so he led the two of clubs! The declarer, Marcel Peeters, one of France's experts, was completely taken in.

The full distribution was:

Dealer: South
Vulnerable: Both

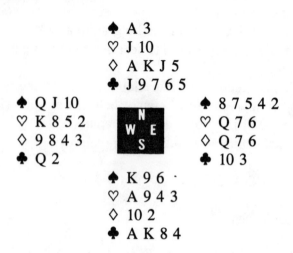

```
                ♠ A 3
                ♡ J 10
                ◇ A K J 5
                ♣ J 9 7 6 5
  ♠ Q J 10                    ♠ 8 7 5 4 2
  ♡ K 8 5 2        N          ♡ Q 7 6
  ◇ 9 8 4 3      W   E        ◇ Q 7 6
  ♣ Q 2            S          ♣ 10 3
                ♠ K 9 6 ·
                ♡ A 9 4 3
                ◇ 10 2
                ♣ A K 8 4
```

Declarer played low from the dummy and took the ten with the king. Feeling perfectly confident, Peeters crossed to dummy's ace of spades and led a club to the eight. Del Duca won with the queen, exited in spades and the slam had evaporated.

To give the declarer his due, Peeters congratulated del Duca on the brilliant lead, and the next morning he telephoned José le Dentu to ensure that the hand would receive worldwide publicity.

Another deceptive trump lead is a low card from king doubleton when you are sure dummy has the ace and the opponents have at least nine trumps between them.

It is particularly effective against a grand slam; and here is an example from an Argentinian National Championship. Luis Attaguile, who has represented his country on many occasions, was holding

♠ K 2   ♡ J 5 4 2   ◇ 8 7 6 4 3   ♣ 10 9

and heard the opponents bid as follows:

West	North	East	South
	2NT	Pass	3♠ (a)
Pass	4♠	Pass	4NT (b)
Pass	5◇ (c)	Pass	7♠
Pass	Pass	Pass	

(a) Natural
(b) Roman Blackwood
(c) One or four aces

Virtually certain that the ace of trumps was on his left, Attaguile led the two of spades.

This was the complete deal:

Dealer: North
Vulnerable: East-West

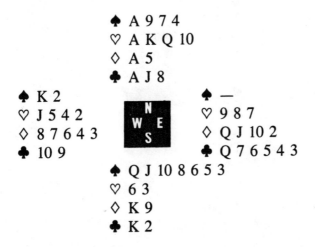

```
                    ♠ A 9 7 4
                    ♡ A K Q 10
                    ◇ A 5
                    ♣ A J 8
    ♠ K 2                          ♠ —
    ♡ J 5 4 2         N            ♡ 9 8 7
    ◇ 8 7 6 4 3    W     E         ◇ Q J 10 2
    ♣ 10 9            S            ♣ Q 7 6 5 4 3
                    ♠ Q J 10 8 6 5 3
                    ♡ 6 3
                    ◇ K 9
                    ♣ K 2
```

With a combined holding of 11 cards in the trump suit, declarer *may* have played for the drop anyway (the odds favoring that play by two percent), but the opening lead persuaded him that the trumps were divided 1-1. Confidently he played the ace of spades from the dummy and when East showed out the grand slam had perished.

My second example comes from the 1975 Cannes Bridge

Festival. It is an enjoyable week, usually held in May just before the famous Film Festival; and the evenings feature a Bridgerama match between Italy and France. This was board 56:

Dealer: East
Vulnerable: Both

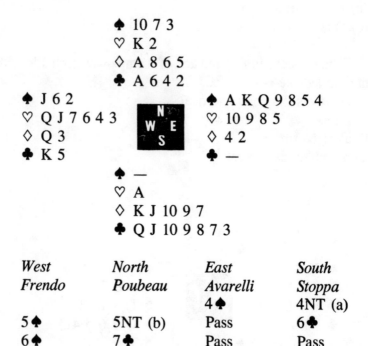

```
              ♠ 10 7 3
              ♡ K 2
              ◇ A 8 6 5
              ♣ A 6 4 2
♠ J 6 2                      ♠ A K Q 9 8 5 4
♡ Q J 7 6 4 3               ♡ 10 9 8 5
◇ Q 3                        ◇ 4 2
♣ K 5                        ♣ —
              ♠ —
              ♡ A
              ◇ K J 10 9 7
              ♣ Q J 10 9 8 7 3
```

West	North	East	South
Frendo	*Poubeau*	*Avarelli*	*Stoppa*
		4♠	4NT (a)
5♠	5NT (b)	Pass	6♣
6♠	7♣	Pass	Pass
Double	Pass	Pass	Pass

(a) Long, strong minors.
(b) Pick your minor-suit slam.

Paul Frendo led a spade, which Jean-Paul Stoppa ruffed. Declarer took the club finesse, dropped the queen of diamonds and claimed his grand slam for plus 2330. *"Pas mal,"* was probably the comment of Dominique Poubeau.

In the other room, the auction reached 6◇ by South, Massimo d'Alelio. At this point Paul Chemla, East, made a Lightner double requesting an unusual lead. West, Michel

Lebel, huddled for a long time, passed and led the five of clubs! D'Alelio played safe by putting on dummy's two, and Chemla's ruff was the only defensive trick. That gave Italy 1540 but France scored 13 IMPs.

At the time Frendo was severely self-critical, stating that he should have taken out insurance by bidding 7♠ (in which case Italy would have gained 10 IMPs), or smoothly led the five of clubs (after which he felt Italy would have profited to the tune of 17 points).

The next deal was originally published in the April 1983 issue of *Australian Bridge*, and was the joint winner of the *Canberra Times* Brilliancy Prize at the *Sitmar* Summer Festival of Bridge, held annually in Canberra in January. This was board 20 from the qualifying round of the National Open Teams Championship.

Dealer: South
Vulnerable: Both

```
                    ♠ K Q J 7 6 2
                    ♡ A Q 8 7
                    ◇ —
                    ♣ 6 5 3
    ♠ 8 5 3                         ♠ 4
    ♡ K 3            N              ♡ 6 5
    ◇ Q 10 5 2     W   E            ◇ K J 8 7 4 3
    ♣ Q 10 9 7       S              ♣ K J 8 4
                    ♠ A 10 9
                    ♡ J 10 9 4 2
                    ◇ A 9 6
                    ♣ A 2
```

West	North	East	South
			1 ♡
Pass	3 ♡	Pass	4 ♣
Pass	4 ◇	Pass	4 ♠
Pass	5NT	Pass	6 ♡
Pass	7 ♡	Pass	Pass
Pass			

3 ♡ was, of course, forcing, after which there were three cuebids. At that point North invoked the Grand Slam Force. However, though both North and South were good players, they were not an established partnership, so North was not sure if his partner was promising or denying a top honor with his 6 ♡ response. Deciding the grand slam would be on a finesse at the worst, he bid seven.

With the finesse right, the grand slam was destined to succeed . . . except that West, Phil Ryan, was able to draw the right conclusion from North's answers to his queries about the auction. He led the three of hearts.

Declarer knew it was possible West was underleading the king, but eventually he decided it was more likely that the lead was from ♡653 than from the king, so he rose with the ace and went down.

Bobby Wolff told me an amusing story concerning this particular deceptive lead. He was playing in a mixed pairs event with a pupil. The opposition bid vigorously to a slam, and Wolff led the four from king-four doubleton in trumps as dummy was marked with the ace.

"At no time was I in danger of losing my trick if partner held the trump queen because I knew she would play it if the dummy followed low. This happened to be the case and there appeared to be no story. But look what happened to poor Bobby Nail. Playing with an expert partner, he made the same opening lead, but when dummy played low she did *not* put up her trump queen. Thus declarer, holding jack-ten-fourth opposite ace-nine-fifth, conceded no trump trick."

It is rubber bridge with neither side vulnerable, and sitting West you hold

♠ Q J 3 2   ♡ K 4   ◇ J 6   ♣ A 7 6 5 2

The auction proceeds:

West	North	East	South
			1 ♡
Pass	2 ♡	Pass	2NT
Pass	4 ♡	Pass	Pass
Pass			

What is your opening lead?

This hand occurred in the earliest days of contract bridge. Playing West was Albert Morehead, who was the first bridge columnist for *The New York Times* and, *inter alia,* a leading lexicographer. Even though it was unlikely the ace of hearts was coming down in the dummy, Morehead decided to lead the four of hearts!

This was the full deal:

Dealer: South
Vulnerable: None

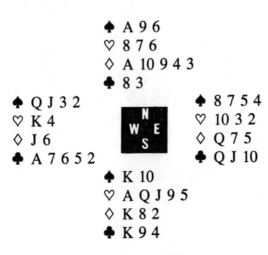

```
                    ♠ A 9 6
                    ♡ 8 7 6
                    ◇ A 10 9 4 3
                    ♣ 8 3
   ♠ Q J 3 2                          ♠ 8 7 5 4
   ♡ K 4              N               ♡ 10 3 2
   ◇ J 6           W   E              ◇ Q 7 5
   ♣ A 7 6 5 2        S               ♣ Q J 10
                    ♠ K 10
                    ♡ A Q J 9 5
                    ◇ K 8 2
                    ♣ K 9 4
```

The declarer is in danger of losing one heart, one diamond and two clubs; and note that any side-suit lead would cost a trick, allowing the game to make. After the actual heart lead, declarer could have made his contract by guessing the position, but why should he? In fact he won East's ten with the jack, crossed to the ace of spades and ran the eight of hearts. Morehead won with the king and was able to return the queen of spades. Declarer drew trumps, but in the fullness of time East gained the lead in diamonds and switched to the queen of clubs to defeat the contract.

The observant reader will have noticed that the declarer could have done better. He should have played a trump to the queen on the second round, retaining the five in his hand. That would have given him an extra dummy entry and permitted him to duck a diamond to West; but it does not detract from Morehead's imaginative lead.

Another deceptive possibility came up when I was partnering Edith in the 1971 Mexican Mixed Pairs Championship. I was sitting West with

♠ 10 4   ♡ A Q 6   ◇ J 7 3   ♣ 8 7 5 4 3

and heard an auction of

West	North	East	South
			2♣ (a)
Pass	2◇ (b)	Pass	2♡
Pass	4♣ (c)	Pass	4NT (d)
Pass	5◇ (e)	Pass	6♡
Pass	Pass	Pass	

(a) Strong
(b) Waiting
(c) Splinter bid with heart support
(d) Roman Key Card Blackwood
(e) One of the five key cards

What would you lead?

I decided upon the ace of hearts, planning to continue with the six if the king appeared in the dummy, otherwise to revert to another suit and await the setting trick with the queen of hearts.

This was the actual full deal:

Dealer: South
Vulnerable: North-South

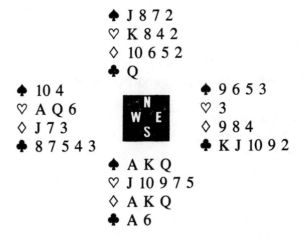

```
                    ♠ J 8 7 2
                    ♡ K 8 4 2
                    ◇ 10 6 5 2
                    ♣ Q
    ♠ 10 4                          ♠ 9 6 5 3
    ♡ A Q 6            N            ♡ 3
    ◇ J 7 3        W     E          ◇ 9 8 4
    ♣ 8 7 5 4 3       S             ♣ K J 10 9 2
                    ♠ A K Q
                    ♡ J 10 9 7 5
                    ◇ A K Q
                    ♣ A 6
```

Declarer confidently put up dummy's king at trick two, thinking I had led from ♡A6. Edith told me afterwards she wished a photographer had been present to catch the expression on declarer's face!

Once more, declarer was given an option he would not have exercised if left to himself. The percentage play for one loser in this suit is to run the jack on the first round.

This particular deceptive play can sometimes be employed at a lower level. This time sitting West was Phillip Alder, who formerly edited the British *Bridge Magazine* (now *Bridge International*) but now is doing freelance bridge writing in the United States from a base in New York City. The deal arose during a Gold Cup match, the premier team event in Great Britain.

With both sides vulnerable, Alder was holding

♠ A Q 6   ♡ A 6   ◇ Q 8 7 4   ♣ 9 6 5 3

The bidding went:

West	North	East	South
			1NT (a)
Pass	2♣	Pass	2◇
Pass	3◇ (b)	Pass	3♠ (c)
Pass	Pass	Pass	

(a) 12-14 points
(b) Asking for three-card majors
(c) Minimum with three spades and two hearts

What would you have led?

Knowing that declarer was also 3-2 in the majors, Alder led the ace of spades.

This was the full deal:

Dealer: South
Vulnerable: Both

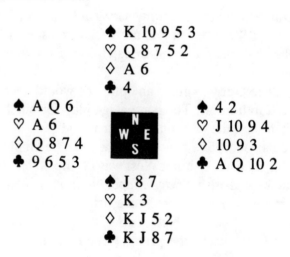

After the ace and another spade, declarer naturally rose with the king and played a heart to his king. West won with the ace, cashed the queen of spades and returned another heart. Declarer was now booked for a two-trick defeat, losing two spades, three hearts and a club.

In the other room Alder's teammates stopped in 2♠ and made it, thus gaining seven IMPs.

Once more, I shall end a chapter with a deal featuring Mike Passell. This one occurred during the qualifying rounds of the 1977 Bermuda Bowl in Manila.

He was sitting West, holding

♠ Q 7 5 4   ♡ 6 3 2   ◊ J 7 5   ♣ Q 6 4

and heard the following auction:

West	North	East	South
			1♣
Pass	1♡	Pass	1♠
Pass	3♠ (a)	Pass	4NT (b)
Pass	5♡	Pass	5NT (b)
Pass	6◊	Pass	7♠
Pass	Pass	Pass	

(a) Forcing
(b) Straightforward Blackwood

What would be your lead?

It sounds like you have to hope to make a trick with your queen of spades, and therefore I expect at the table you would have made a red-suit lead and tried to look uninterested in the proceedings. Passell led a trump!

This was the hand:

Dealer: South
Vulnerable: None

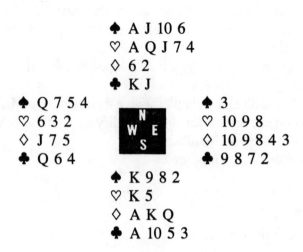

```
                    ♠ A J 10 6
                    ♡ A Q J 7 4
                    ◊ 6 2
                    ♣ K J
   ♠ Q 7 5 4                        ♠ 3
   ♡ 6 3 2          N               ♡ 10 9 8
   ◊ J 7 5       W     E            ◊ 10 9 8 4 3
   ♣ Q 6 4          S               ♣ 9 8 7 2
                    ♠ K 9 8 2
                    ♡ K 5
                    ◊ A K Q
                    ♣ A 10 5 3
```

On the spade lead, the declarer put in dummy's ten and, when it held, followed with the ace. Imagine his shock when *East* discarded! Perhaps declarer should have continued with a low spade at trick two, proposing to finesse the eight if East followed(!), but when a defender finds such an imaginative lead, one cannot help feeling he deserves to break the contract.

Without a trump lead declarer is likely to play West for the missing queen. Because one normally wishes to give nothing away and it is reasonable to expect the declarer's combined trump holding to be solid, the textbooks recommend leading a trump against grand-slam contracts. And when the opening lead is not a trump but away from a weak holding in a side suit, there is a suggestion that West is looking at a holding in trumps that makes it an unattractive choice — viz, the queen.

In the other room Passell's teammates stopped in six and so the difference between making and defeating the grand slam was a cool 25 IMPs; you win 14 or lose 11.

Chapter 6

PASSIVE LEADS

Nor less I deem that there are Powers
Which of themselves our mind impress;
That we can feed this mind of ours
In a wise passiveness.

EXPOSTULATION AND REPLY, WILLIAM WORDSWORTH

The final chapter focuses attention on the bread-and-butter of trump leads: the desire for a passive start to the defense. Some of the time you are confronted with an opening-lead situation against a trump contract where, for some reason or other, all side-suit leads appear dangerous. An attacking lead is not appetizing, and so you have to fall back on a trump as a 'safe' start.

The classic example, as I mentioned at the end of the previous chapter, is a trump lead against a grand slam. In a club duplicate I held the following hand sitting West:

♠ 8 4 3 2   ♡ 7 5 3   ◇ 9 8 7   ♣ J 5 4

The bidding proceeded:

West	North	East	South
			2♣ (a)
Pass	2♠ (b)	Pass	3♡
Pass	4♡	Pass	7♡
Pass	Pass	Pass	

(a) Artificial game-force
(b) Three controls (A = 2; K = 1)

131

What would you lead?

Your choice, of course, is a trump. It is practically certain that declarer has no trump loser, and if he needs a finesse in a side suit, let him do his own work — why risk saving him a guess?

These were the four hands:

Dealer: South
Vulnerable: None

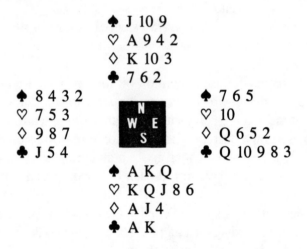

```
                ♠ J 10 9
                ♡ A 9 4 2
                ◇ K 10 3
                ♣ 7 6 2
  ♠ 8 4 3 2                    ♠ 7 6 5
  ♡ 7 5 3          N           ♡ 10
  ◇ 9 8 7      W       E       ◇ Q 6 5 2
  ♣ J 5 4          S           ♣ Q 10 9 8 3
                ♠ A K Q
                ♡ K Q J 8 6
                ◇ A J 4
                ♣ A K
```

After drawing trumps and eliminating the black suits in the hope of getting a count on the hand, declarer was faced with a two-way finesse for the queen of diamonds. He got it wrong and so went one down.

By the way, declarer should have guessed the location of the queen of diamonds as East showed up with only one heart to West's three. Therefore West has only ten unknown cards to East's twelve unknown cards and thus the odds were 12 to 10 that East had the queen of diamonds.

With neither side vulnerable, you pick up

♠ J 8 7 3   ♡ A Q 8 7   ◇ 4   ♣ 10 7 5 2

The dealer on your right opens with 6 ◊ (!) and his partner raises to seven. What is your opening lead?

This hand occurred during the match between Great Britain and Hungary in the 1981 European Championships in Birmingham, England. At both tables the bidding went as described, and the two Wests, Paul Hackett and Miklos Dumbovich, chose to lead the ace of hearts.

This was not a wise choice, a trump clearly being indicated, and justice was seen to be done when the full deal proved to be:

Dealer: South
Vulnerable: None

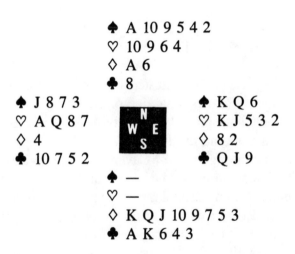

```
                    ♠ A 10 9 5 4 2
                    ♡ 10 9 6 4
                    ◊ A 6
                    ♣ 8
   ♠ J 8 7 3                          ♠ K Q 6
   ♡ A Q 8 7          N              ♡ K J 5 3 2
   ◊ 4            W       E          ◊ 8 2
   ♣ 10 7 5 2         S              ♣ Q J 9
                    ♠ —
                    ♡ —
                    ◊ K Q J 10 9 7 5 3
                    ♣ A K 6 4 3
```

After the heart leads, the declarers were able to ruff two clubs in the dummy and discard the third on the ace of spades to make their grand slams. A trump lead, of course, defeats the contract.

The next example makes an interesting declarer-play problem.

133

Dealer: North
Vulnerable: North-South

♠ K Q 7
♡ K J 10 9 5 2
◊ J 7
♣ 10 3

♠ A J 9 8 6
♡ A
◊ A Q 3 2
♣ A J 4

You are in 6♠ after an uncontested auction, and West leads the two of spades. What is your line of attack?

How would you have played differently if West had led the six of clubs, East putting up the king?

This hand arose during the 1981 Cavendish Club Invitational Calcutta Pairs Championship held in New York City every May. For the winners, Tommy Sanders, partnering Lou Bluhm, led a trump and the declarer failed to find the best (and winning) line of taking the first trick in hand, cashing the ace of hearts, entering dummy with a trump and running the jack of hearts, discarding a minor-suit card if East does not cover with the queen. As long as trumps are 3-2 and West does not ruff this trick, declarer is safe.

The actual full deal was:

Dealer: North
Vulnerable: North-South

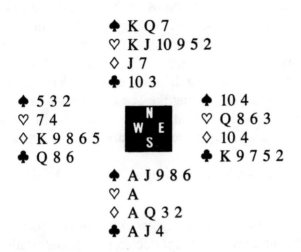

```
                    ♠ K Q 7
                    ♡ K J 10 9 5 2
                    ◇ J 7
                    ♣ 10 3
        ♠ 5 3 2              ♠ 10 4
        ♡ 7 4          N     ♡ Q 8 6 3
        ◇ K 9 8 6 5  W   E   ◇ 10 4
        ♣ Q 8 6        S     ♣ K 9 7 5 2
                    ♠ A J 9 8 6
                    ♡ A
                    ◇ A Q 3 2
                    ♣ A J 4
```

At the table where a club was led, the declarer was world
champion Judi Radin. She was partnering Kathie Wei, who does
so much for bridge and is married to C. C., the inventor of
the Precision system. They did extremely well to finish second
in such a strong event.

They were playing against a top New York pair, David
Berkowitz and Harold Lilie, who came in third. The reason
Berkowitz led a club rather than a trump was because of the
bidding, which had gone:

West	North	East	South
Berkowitz	Wei	Lilie	Radin
	Pass	Pass	1♣
Pass	1♡	Pass	1♠
Pass	2♠	Pass	3♣
Pass	3♠	Pass	6♠
Pass	Pass	Pass	

1♣ was strong, promising at least 16 points; and 1♡ was
a game-forcing positive response. Berkowitz asked himself why

Radin had bothered to bid 3 ♣, came to the conclusion that she was trying to stop a club lead, and therefore led one! However, the appearance of the ten of clubs in dummy proved to be a lifesaver for declarer. She won the king of clubs with the ace, cashed the ace of hearts and played back a club. West won with the queen and switched to a trump, but it was too late. Radin won in her hand, discarded a diamond on the jack of clubs and cross-ruffed the hand, cashing the ace of diamonds and king of hearts *en route*. (Maybe next time this situation arises, Radin will bid 3 ◊ instead. The psychology of bridge is so fascinating.)

Passive trump leads often fulfill additional tasks. Here are some possibilities:

a. They may prematurely knock out a vital entry from the dummy or disrupt declarer's communications
b. They may cut down on ruffing power
c. In the case of the lead of the ace of trumps, it may serve one of several purposes

Here is an instructive hand Edith held in a game at our local club in Mexico that exhibits point *a* above. The opponents were playing Precision, and she was sitting West with

♠ 8 5   ♡ Q 8 6 4   ◊ A 9 7 2   ♣ K 8 3

The auction proceeded:

West	North	East	South
			1 ♠
Pass	1NT (a)	Pass	3 ♠ (b)
Pass	Pass	Pass	

(a) Forcing
(b) A good suit but less than 16 points

Judging any other lead to be too dangerous, Edith selected the five of spades.

This was the full deal:

Dealer: South
Vulnerable: None

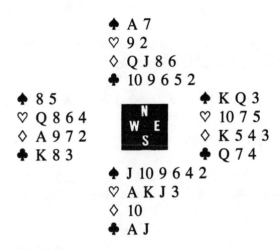

```
                    ♠ A 7
                    ♡ 9 2
                    ◊ Q J 8 6
                    ♣ 10 9 6 5 2
♠ 8 5                               ♠ K Q 3
♡ Q 8 6 4          N                ♡ 10 7 5
◊ A 9 7 2        W   E              ◊ K 5 4 3
♣ K 8 3            S                ♣ Q 7 4
                    ♠ J 10 9 6 4 2
                    ♡ A K J 3
                    ◊ 10
                    ♣ A J
```

First consider all the side-suit leads. A heart is into the ace-king-jack and gives declarer an easy nine tricks.

The ace of diamonds, even if followed by a trump switch, allows declarer to rise with the ace of spades, take the ruffing diamond finesse, reenter dummy with a heart ruff and discard his club or heart loser.

A psychic low diamond lead does not work. Even if East puts up the king and switches to a club, declarer ruffs both his heart losers in the dummy.

Finally, a club sets up a trick in that suit and the contract makes.

But look at the effect of a trump lead. The vital ace-of-spades entry was removed prematurely and at the same time a possible additional heart ruff was neutralized.

Declarer took the reasonable line of trying the heart finesse after winning the first trick with the ace of spades, and so ended two down, giving East-West a top.

(Just a brief footnote on the bidding: it is better for South to rebid 2 ♡ over the forcing notrump response. He should try to find a fit in either major, not just rely on the extra length in spades. If North held, for example

♠ 5   ♡ Q 10 7 6 5   ◊ A 6 4   ♣ 6 4 3 2

he would pass 3 ♠, but 4 ♡ is a heavy favorite to make.)

With both sides vulnerable, you hold

♠ K Q 9 8   ♡ K 10 4   ◊ J 5   ♣ 8 7 3 2

and the auction goes as follows:

West	North	East	South
Granovetter	Bergen	Rosenberg	Cohen
			1 ◊
Pass	1 ♡	Pass	2 ♣
Pass	3 ♣	Pass	4 ◊ (a)
Pass	4NT (b)	Pass	6 ♣
Pass	Pass	Pass	

(a) Roman Key Card Blackwood
(b) Two of the five key cards but no queen of clubs

What is your opening lead? Would it make any difference if they had stopped in 5 ♣?

It is fairly clear that South must have a distributional hand to bid first a non-forcing 2 ♣ and then to blast into a slam when his partner shows support and moderate values. Matt Granovetter judged that this meant it was right to lead a trump, not the king of spades, and he was proved correct when the full deal turned out to be:

Dealer: South
Vulnerable: Both

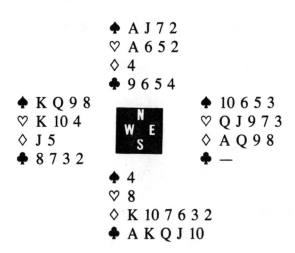

```
                  ♠ A J 7 2
                  ♡ A 6 5 2
                  ◊ 4
                  ♣ 9 6 5 4
  ♠ K Q 9 8                      ♠ 10 6 5 3
  ♡ K 10 4          N            ♡ Q J 9 7 3
  ◊ J 5          W     E         ◊ A Q 9 8
  ♣ 8 7 3 2         S            ♣ —
                  ♠ 4
                  ♡ 8
                  ◊ K 10 7 6 3 2
                  ♣ A K Q J 10
```

Larry Cohen won the trump lead in hand, entered dummy with a spade to the ace and led the four of diamonds. Because of the bad trump break, East, Michael Rosenberg, could have defeated the contract by rising with the ace, but he knew it was better to play low. Declarer won with the king, ruffed a diamond, played a trump to hand and led another diamond, ruffing with dummy's last trump. However, now the hand was out of control and Cohen finished two down.

In the other room the contract was only 5♣ but West led the king of spades. This allowed declarer to win in the dummy and play a diamond immediately. Even though East ducked, South was in control. He won with the king, ruffed a diamond, returned to hand with a trump, ruffed another diamond, drew trumps, and conceded the ace of diamonds to East, thus registering an overtrick. Granovetter's team gained 13 IMPs.

The deal arose during the 1986 Cavendish Teams Championship which follows the Calcutta Pairs mentioned above. The Granovetter team of himself, his wife Pam, Jimmy Cayne, Zia Mahmood and Rosenberg won by over a match with a score of almost 78 percent. And that followed on the heels of a win in the Pairs by Granovetter and Rosenberg.

With both sides vulnerable, you hold

♠ Q 10 4   ♡ 8 4   ◇ 9 7 2   ♣ K Q 10 8 3

The auction contains an unusual gadget:

West	North	East	South
			1NT
Pass	3◇ (a)	Pass	3♡
Pass	4♡	Pass	4NT
Pass	5♡ (b)	Pass	6♡
Pass	Pass	Pass	

(a) 4-4-1-4 shape and game-forcing values
(b) Two aces

What is your opening lead?

In Chapter 1 there was a hand where a side-suit lead was needed to break up a squeeze. Rather rarer, but still possible, is the situation when a trump lead serves this purpose.

This was the full deal:

Dealer: South
Vulnerable: Both

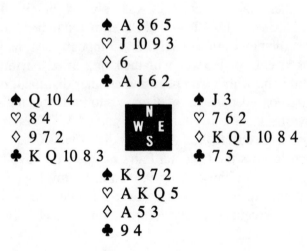

♠ A 8 6 5
♡ J 10 9 3
◇ 6
♣ A J 6 2

♠ Q 10 4
♡ 8 4
◇ 9 7 2
♣ K Q 10 8 3

♠ J 3
♡ 7 6 2
◇ K Q J 10 8 4
♣ 7 5

♠ K 9 7 2
♡ A K Q 5
◇ A 5 3
♣ 9 4

At the table in fact East had perhaps inadvisedly doubled 3 ◇, so West led that suit; but the declarer, Mike Passell, still had to play for a specific distribution to take 12 tricks. He won the first trick and played a club, ducking when West went in with the queen. (If you would have led the king of clubs at trick one, declarer would have ducked to produce the same position.) West played back a club, and the jack was finessed successfully. A trump to hand, a diamond ruff, another trump to hand and a second diamond ruff was followed by a spade to the king to give this position:

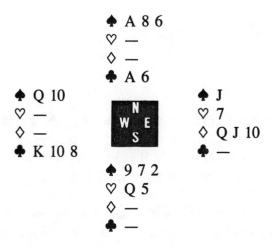

Two rounds of trumps squeezed West in the black suits; and gained 13 IMPs because they stopped in game in the other room.

If West had led a trump initially and continued with a second one when given his club trick, declarer's communications would have been left in tatters and the slam would have failed.

b. Even when declarer seems to have a self-sufficient suit and dummy holds only a singleton or doubleton, a trump lead might kill a ruff.

With neither side vulnerable, you hold

♠ J 3   ♡ 8 7 6 4   ◇ Q J 10 3   ♣ Q 8 6

The bidding proceeds:

West	North	East	South
Pass	Pass	Pass	2♣ (a)
Pass	3♣ (b)	Pass	4NT (c)
Pass	5◇ (d)	Pass	7♠
Pass	Pass	Pass	

(a) Game-forcing
(b) The ace of clubs and no other ace
(c) Asking for kings
(d) One king

What is your lead?

The deal occurred in France, where they call the opening bid Albarran after one of the greatest of their players, Pierre Albarran, who died in 1960. He invented the idea of ace-showing responses over 2♣ opening bids (and also canapé-bidding: showing a shorter suit before a longer one.)

At the time West settled for the safe-looking queen of diamonds, but it turned out to be ineffective when the full deal proved to be:

```
Dealer: West        ♠ 2
Vulnerable: None    ♡ J 9 5 3 2
                    ◇ 5
                    ♣ A K 9 7 5 4
    ♠ J 3                         ♠ 7 4
    ♡ 8 7 6 4         N           ♡ K 10
    ◇ Q J 10 3      W   E         ◇ 9 7 6 4 2
    ♣ Q 8 6           S           ♣ J 10 3 2
                    ♠ A K Q 10 9 8 6 5
                    ♡ A Q
                    ◇ A K 8
                    ♣ —
```

The hand was reported by José le Dentu in the French magazine, *Le Bridgeur*. After the diamond lead, declarer had no trouble. But a trump lead, of course, would have written a different story.

I am sure you chose to lead a trump, but did you select the three or the jack? Here it would not have mattered, but if dummy had had a singleton which your partner could not beat, you would have regretted leading the three rather than the jack.

This time you can have a defensive problem to consider. Only your side is vulnerable, and the auction is both conventional and explosive.

West	North	East	South
	2 ♣ (a)	Pass	2 ◇ (b)
2 ♡	3 ♣	3 ♡	6 ◇
Pass	Pass	Pass	

(a) Precision: 12-15 points, five or more clubs
(b) A relay asking for further definition

Your partner leads the four of diamonds, and this is what you can see:

Dealer: North
Vulnerable: East-West

```
          ♠ 5 3
          ♡ K Q 9 4
          ◇ 8
          ♣ K Q 10 5 4 2
                        ♠ A 10 9 6 4
              N         ♡ 10 5 2
           W     E      ◇ —
              S         ♣ A J 9 7 6
```

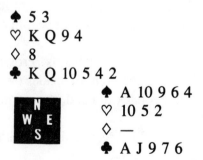

Dummy's eight of diamonds holds the first trick while you discard the two of hearts; and next comes the three of spades from the dummy. How do you plan the defense?

Dealer: North
Vulnerable: East-West

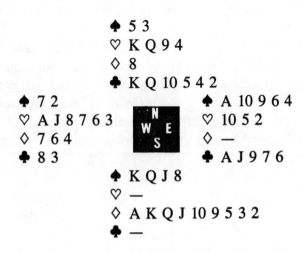

                    ♠ 5 3
                    ♡ K Q 9 4
                    ◇ 8
                    ♣ K Q 10 5 4 2
    ♠ 7 2   ♠ A 10 9 6 4
    ♡ A J 8 7 6 3   ♡ 10 5 2
    ◇ 7 6 4   ◇ —
    ♣ 8 3   ♣ A J 9 7 6
                    ♠ K Q J 8
                    ♡ —
                    ◇ A K Q J 10 9 5 3 2
                    ♣ —

East must put in the nine or ten to stop declarer finessing the eight. Did you find that play? I agree it is possible(!) declarer will not adopt this line of play, preferring to run eight rounds of diamonds in the hope of a misdefense (which should not occur here), but how delightful to guarantee defeating a contract with a play like that!

In real life, West was a little unlucky when he led the ace of hearts, though he might have asked himself why South had failed to use Blackwood. Also, he did not have the advantage of knowing his hand was going to appear in a book about trump leads.

Declarer ruffed the ace of hearts, crossed to the eight of diamonds, discarded the eight of spades on the king of hearts, ruffed a heart to get back to hand, drew trumps and conceded a spade trick.

You return to the West seat, and with neither side vulnerable you are holding

♠ 6 2   ♡ Q 9 7 5   ◇ K 3 2   ♣ K 8 4 3

The opponents' auction takes a slow but steady road to the
six-level:

West	North	East	South
Pass	Pass	Pass	2♣
Pass	2◇	Pass	2♠
Pass	3◇	Pass	3♠
Pass	3NT	Pass	4♡
Pass	4♠	Pass	5♠
Pass	6♠	Pass	Pass
Pass			

After the strong and artificial 2♣ opener and the negative
2◇ response, the rest of the auction is natural. What is your
lead?

This time probably you would have come up with a trump
without any help because all the other leads look so dangerous.

At trick one I doubt partner was overly enamored of your
choice, but it proved to be the killer. The full deal was:

Dealer: West
Vulnerable: None

```
                    ♠ 10
                    ♡ 10 4
                    ◇ Q 9 8 7 5
                    ♣ A Q J 7 2
   ♠ 6 2                          ♠ K 9
   ♡ Q 9 7 5          N           ♡ J 6 2
   ◇ K 3 2         W     E        ◇ J 10 6 4
   ♣ K 8 4 3          S           ♣ 10 9 6 5
                    ♠ A Q J 8 7 5 4 3
                    ♡ A K 8 3
                    ◇ A
                    ♣ —
```

The hand occurred during the 1983 Australian Trials. Sitting West was Sue Hobley, who has represented Australia, *inter alia,* in the 1981 and 1985 Venice Cup competitions; and East was Roelof Smilde, one of Australia's best players and an international on many occasions.

Declarer won the first trick with the ace of spades and started running the trumps. Smilde played high-low in both minors to give his partner the count, and after the last spade the position was:

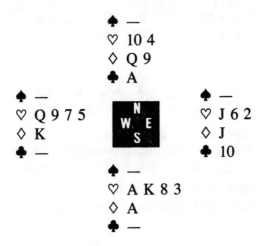

Declarer cashed the ace-king of hearts, East playing low. Next came the ace of diamonds followed by a low heart. However, Sue Hobley was up to the test: she rose with the queen of hearts to swallow her partner's jack and made the last trick with the nine of hearts. A lovely example of the Crocodile Coup.

In the other room the same contract was reached and the play was similar except that East discarded a heart on the run of the spades. This gave the declarer a chance to make his contract by cashing both red-suit aces and then exiting with a low heart, endplaying whichever defender took the trick, but he failed to find the play and went one down.

Now on to point *c* above, leading the ace of trumps. That could serve one of three purposes:

1. To enable you to look at the dummy before deciding up your next play.

2. To allow you to draw at least two rounds of trumps immediately.

3. To remove the singleton ace from your hand so that you cannot be endplayed with it later in the play.

Neither side is vulnerable, and you are sitting in the West chair that was originally occupied by an Egyptian taking part in a rubber-bridge game in Monte Carlo. Your hand is

♠ 6 4   ♡ A Q 3 2   ◇ K Q 9 8   ♣ K 7 5

and the auction proceeds:

West	North	East	South
1 ♡	Pass	1 ♠	2 ♡
Pass	3 ♣	Pass	3 ♡
Double	4 ♣	Pass	Pass
Double	Pass	Pass	4 ♡
Double	Pass	Pass	Pass

Probably you do not agree with all of your actions, but now it is time to decide upon your opening lead. What would your choice have been at the table?

Given the introduction, you probably selected the ace of hearts. The dummy comes down, and this is what you can see:

Dealer: West
Vulnerable: None

```
                    ♠ 8 5
                    ♡ 10 5
                    ◊ 10
                    ♣ A Q 10 8 6 4 3 2
        ♠ 6 4              N
        ♡ A Q 3 2       W     E
        ◊ K Q 9 8          S
        ♣ K 7 5
```

Partner discards the two of diamonds on the first trick. What do you do now?

Your best chance to defeat the contract is to hope that declarer is void in clubs, which is likely as partner is unlikely to have 12 or 13 cards in spades and diamonds and have passed over 3♣. You should continue with the queen of hearts, dramatically sacrificing a trump trick but getting two diamonds and a spade in return.

In real life West made the obvious-looking opening lead of the king of diamonds but that left declarer with no problem when the full deal proved to be:

Dealer: West
Vulnerable: None

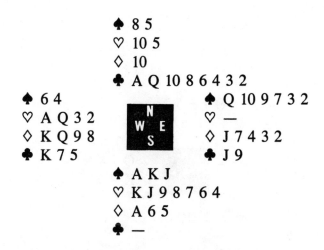

```
              ♠ 8 5
              ♡ 10 5
              ◊ 10
              ♣ A Q 10 8 6 4 3 2
  ♠ 6 4                        ♠ Q 10 9 7 3 2
  ♡ A Q 3 2         N          ♡ —
  ◊ K Q 9 8      W     E       ◊ J 7 4 3 2
  ♣ K 7 5          S           ♣ J 9
              ♠ A K J
              ♡ K J 9 8 7 6 4
              ◊ A 6 5
              ♣ —
```

Declarer won the opening lead with the ace, ruffed a diamond, discarded the jack of spades on the ace of clubs, crossed
to the ace of spades, ruffed his last diamond and conceded the
ace-queen of trumps to register an overtrick.

With only your side vulnerable, you hold

♠ J 9 3 2   ♡ A K 10 7 6 4 2   ◊ 10   ♣ A

and all four players join in the bidding:

West	North	East	South
	Pass	Pass	1♣
1♡	3♣	3♡	6♣
Pass	Pass	Pass	

What is our opening lead?

This was the full deal:

Dealer: North
Vulnerable: East-West

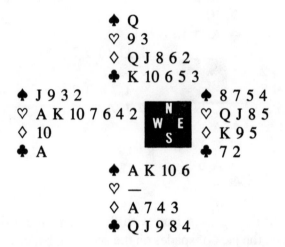

```
                    ♠ Q
                    ♡ 9 3
                    ◊ Q J 8 6 2
                    ♣ K 10 6 5 3
        ♠ J 9 3 2                      ♠ 8 7 5 4
        ♡ A K 10 7 6 4 2               ♡ Q J 8 5
        ◊ 10                           ◊ K 9 5
        ♣ A                            ♣ 7 2
                    ♠ A K 10 6
                    ♡ —
                    ◊ A 7 4 3
                    ♣ Q J 9 8 4
```

If West had led the ace of clubs, declarer would have been doomed to defeat. But at the time West chose the king of hearts, despite the bidding making it virtually certain South was void in the suit. It was not clear that the lead would cost, though, as the obvious line seemed to be to hope that East had the doubleton king of diamonds. However, the declarer saw an extra chance. He ruffed the ace of hearts, crossed to the queen of spades, trumped the nine of hearts, cashed the ace-king of spades, discarding two of dummy's diamonds, ruffed his last spade with the ten of clubs and led the queen of diamonds. Whether or not it was covered, declarer planned to play a trump next. If diamonds were 2-2, he was always home, but if they were 3-1 and the ace of clubs was a singleton, there was a chance that defender would be endplayed, as indeed he was.

Here is another hand where the defender was embarrassed to find the ace of trumps still in his hand.

Dealer: South
Vulnerable: East-West

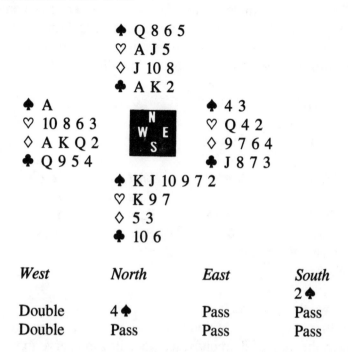

	♠ Q 8 6 5	
	♡ A J 5	
	◊ J 10 8	
	♣ A K 2	

♠ A		♠ 4 3
♡ 10 8 6 3		♡ Q 4 2
◊ A K Q 2		◊ 9 7 6 4
♣ Q 9 5 4		♣ J 8 7 3

	♠ K J 10 9 7 2	
	♡ K 9 7	
	◊ 5 3	
	♣ 10 6	

West	North	East	South
			2 ♠
Double	4 ♠	Pass	Pass
Double	Pass	Pass	Pass

When the responder raises a weak two-bid to game, especially at favorable vulnerability, it could be as an advance sacrifice or with an expectation of success. This can make life difficult for the opponents to judge whose hand it is, especially if they do not use responsive doubles at that level. This explains West's second double; and East just had to hope the contract would fail.

West led the king of diamonds, and followed with two more rounds of the suit. The declarer, Jack Greenberg, the husband of world champion Gail, ruffed and played three rounds of clubs, trumping the last one in hand. Now came the ten of spades from hand, and West was endplayed when he had to win with the ace. He was forced to lead a heart, declarer played low from the dummy and the contract was home.

It will almost always pay you to get rid of that singleton ace of trumps as soon as possible. West's actual lead was reasonable, but the ace of spades should have been cashed before proceeding with the diamonds.

The last two examples feature famous hands. The first comes from the 1967 European Championships in Dublin.

Oscar Bellentani, playing for Italy against Sweden, was sitting third-in-hand at unfavorable vulnerability with

♠ A K 8   ♡ A 10 9 6   ◇ K   ♣ K J 8 7 2

The auction proceeded:

West	North	East	South
	Pass		1 ◇
Double	4 ♠ (a)	Pass	5 ◇
Pass	6 ◇	Pass	Pass
Pass			

(a) Natural

What would you lead?

Without any hints, do you think you would have even considered the king of diamonds, let alone had the nerve to make the lead? This is surely the most spectacular 'passive' trump lead of all time.

The full deal was:

Dealer: East
Vulnerable: East-West

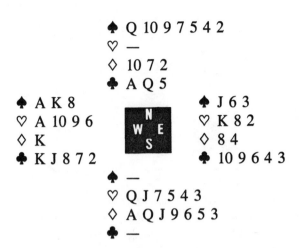

```
              ♠ Q 10 9 7 5 4 2
              ♡ —
              ◊ 10 7 2
              ♣ A Q 5
♠ A K 8                        ♠ J 6 3
♡ A 10 9 6                     ♡ K 8 2
◊ K                            ◊ 8 4
♣ K J 8 7 2                    ♣ 10 9 6 4 3
              ♠ —
              ♡ Q J 7 5 4 3
              ◊ A Q J 9 6 5 3
              ♣ —
```

On any other lead but the king of diamonds, declarer would ruff three hearts in the dummy, drop the singleton king (having no diamonds left in the dummy with which to take the finesse), draw the last trump and concede a heart to make his slam.

Was it second sight or did technique inspire Bellentani's intuition? Undoubtedly it was the latter, something often described as flair. With the bidding indicating wild distribution, any lead was bound to be speculative and might prove catastrophic. But North's raise to 6 ◊ suggested a ruffing value somewhere, so even if the lead of the king cost a trick, it would surely return later in the play.

And the final deal in this book features the person who is reported to have made the statement at the beginning of this book: do not lead trumps . . . unless it is right. The player in question was one of our all-time greats — Lew Mathe, who sadly died in March 1986. Not only did he lead a trump but he followed it up with the most brilliant defense.

Dealer: West
Vulnerable: None

```
                    ♠ 7 6 3
                    ♡ A 9 4
                    ◊ K J 10 9 4 2
                    ♣ 7
   ♠ A 10 8              N
   ♡ 8 7            W         E
   ◊ A Q 8 5 3          S
   ♣ Q 6 4
```

West	North	East	South
West	*North*	*East*	*South*
1 ◊	Pass	1 ♠	2 ♡
2 ♠	3 ♡	Pass	4 ♡
Pass	Pass	Pass	

Mathe led the eight of hearts, declarer went up with dummy's ace, cashed the ace-king of clubs, discarding a spade from dummy, ruffed the eight of clubs in the dummy, trumped a diamond in hand and, at trick six, led the master jack of clubs. How would you defend?

It is fairly clear declarer is proposing to discard another spade on the club winner, so it looks natural to ruff with the apparently worthless seven of hearts. But if declarer still discards, what will you lead next? A diamond will set up the king, and a spade might establish declarer's king; and in both cases South will still be able to organize a spade ruff in dummy. So Mathe discarded a diamond, defeating the contract when the full deal proved to be as he envisaged:

Dealer: West
Vulnerable: None

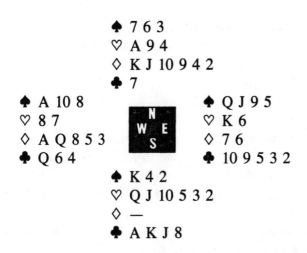

```
              ♠ 7 6 3
              ♡ A 9 4
              ◊ K J 10 9 4 2
              ♣ 7
♠ A 10 8                      ♠ Q J 9 5
♡ 8 7          N              ♡ K 6
◊ A Q 8 5 3  W   E            ◊ 7 6
♣ Q 6 4        S             ♣ 10 9 5 3 2
              ♠ K 4 2
              ♡ Q J 10 5 3 2
              ◊ —
              ♣ A K J 8
```

Declarer threw the six of spades from the dummy and exited with the king of spades. If West did not have another trump, declarer was home, but Mathe produced the seven of hearts, allowing partner to win with the king and cash the queen-jack of spades to defeat the contract.

That is an ideal hand with which to bring down the curtain on this look at trump leads; but by way of a curtain call I would like to repeat that although a trump lead is sometimes the killer, a side-suit lead will be the winner far more often.

And for my encore, here is a tabulated summary of the essential points highlighted during these pages.

DO NOT LEAD A TRUMP IF:

1. You have a useful trump holding.
2. You have a singleton trump and leading it may damage partner's holding.
3. You want to score ruffs:
   - a. in your hand
   - b. in your partner's hand
   - c. in both hands (a cross-ruff).
4. Partner has instructed you to lead a particular suit, often via a lead-directing double.
5. An attacking lead is needed before declarer can take discards.
6. You need to attack an entry, thus destroying declarer's communications.
7. A forcing lead is needed because you or partner have four or more trumps, or declarer is in a tenuous fit that needs to be tapped.

CONSIDER LEADING A TRUMP IF:

1. You want to protect your side's high-card strength, particularly when
   a. partner has shown a strong balanced hand
   b. the opponents have taken a high-level sacrifice with few high cards.
2. You want to stop ruffs, especially when
   a. an opponent has shown a three-suiter or partial three-suiter
   b. the opponents bid all the suits and end up in the fourth
   c. an opponent has insisted on a suit contract despite his partner's suggesting notrump
   d. declarer has been left in his second suit
   e. the third suit bid produced a fit
   f. dummy has exactly three trumps and a ruffing value
   g. dummy is marked with four trumps plus a short suit and an opposing cross-ruff seems likely
   h. an opponent has pulled his partner's penalty double
   i. partner has made a penalty double of a part-score.
3. You want to draw trumps because
   a. partner has passed your take-out double
   b. partner refuses to balance but is marked with strength
   c. you have long trumps (weak or strong).
4. You want to make a deceptive trump lead.
5. A passive defense is indicated.

Finally, as you, the audience, file out of the theater, please do not consider these lists complete. To assume that my research has covered all possibilities would be presumptuous. I believe in the words of François, duc de la Rochefoucauld: ''The true way to be deceived is to think oneself more clever than others.''

THE BEST OF DEVYN PRESS

Bridge Conventions Complete
by Amalya Kearse
$17.95

An undated and expanded edition (over 800 pages) of the reference book no duplicate player can afford to be without. The reviews say it all:

"At last! A book with both use and appeal for expert or novice plus everybody in between. Every partnership will find material they will wish to add to their present system. Not only are all the conventions in use anywhere today clearly and aptly described, but Kearse criticizes various treatments regarding potential flaws and how they can be circumvented.

"Do yourself a favor and add this book to your shelf even if you don't enjoy most bridge books. This book is a treat as well as a classic."
—ACBL BULLETIN

"A must for duplicate fans, this is a comprehensive, well-written guide through the maze of systems and conventions. This should be particularly useful to those who don't want to be taken off guard by an unfamiliar convention, because previously it would have been necessary to amass several references to obtain all the information presented."
—BRIDGE WORLD MAGAZINE

Published January, 1984

Recommended for: all duplicate players

ISBN 0-910791-07-4 paperback

Test Your Play As Declarer, Volume 1
by Jeff Rubens and Paul Lukacs
$5.95

Any reader who studies this book carefully will certainly become much more adept at playing out a hand. There are 89 hands here, each emphasizing a particular point in declarer play. The solution to each problem explains how and why a declarer should handle his hands in a certain way. A reprint of the original.
Published December, 1983

Recommended for: intermediate through expert

ISBN 0-910791-12-0 paperback

Devyn Press Book of Partnership Understandings
by Mike Lawrence
$2.95

Stop bidding misunderstandings before they occur with this valuable guide. It covers all the significant points you should discuss with your partner, whether you are forming a new partnership or you have played together for years.
Published December, 1983

Recommended for: novice through expert

ISBN 0-910791-08-2 paperback

101 Bridge Maxims
by H. W. Kelsey
$7.95

The experience of a master player and writer condensed into 101 easy-to-understand adages. Each hand will help you remember these essential rules during the heat of battle.
Published December, 1983

Recommended for: bright beginner through advanced.

ISBN 0-910791-10-4 paperback

Play Bridge with Mike Lawrence
by Mike Lawrence
$9.95

Follow Mike through a 2-session matchpoint event at a regional tournament, and learn how to gather information from the auction, the play of the cards and the atmosphere at the table. When to go against the field, compete, make close doubles, and more.
Published December, 1983

Recommended for: bright beginner through expert.

ISBN 0-910791-09-0 paperback

Play These Hands With Me
by Terence Reese
$7.95

Studies 60 hands in minute detail. How to analyze your position and sum up information you have available, with a post-mortem reviewing main points.
Published December, 1983

Recommended for: intermediate through expert.

ISBN 0-910791-11-2 paperback

THE BEST OF DEVYN PRESS
Newly Published Bridge Books

THE BEST OF DEVYN PRESS
Bridge Books

A collection of the world's premier bridge authors have produced, for your enjoyment, this wide and impressive selection of books.

MATCHPOINTS
by Kit Woolsey
$9.95

The long-awaited second book by the author of the classic *Partnership Defense*. *Matchpoints* examines all of the crucial aspects of duplicate bridge. It is surprising, with the wealth of excellent books on bidding and play, how neglected matchpoint strategy has been—Kit has filled that gap forever with the best book ever written on the subject. The chapters include: general concepts, constructive bidding, competitive bidding, defensive bidding and the play.
Published October, 1982
Recommended for: intermediate through expert.
ISBN 0-910791-00-7 paperback

DYNAMIC DEFENSE
by Mike Lawrence
$9.95

One of the top authors of the '80's has produced a superior work in his latest effort. These unique hands offer you an over-the-shoulder look at how a World Champion reasons through the most difficult part of bridge. You will improve your technique as you sit at the table and attempt to find the winning sequence of plays. Each of the 65 problems is thoroughly explained and analyzed in the peerless Lawrence style.
Published October, 1982.
Recommended for: bright beginner through expert.
ISBN 0-910791-01-5 paperback

MODERN IDEAS IN BIDDING
by Dr. George Rosenkranz and Alan Truscott
$9.95

Mexico's top player combines with the bridge editor of the New York Times to produce a winner's guide to bidding theory. Constructive bidding, slams, pre-emptive bidding, competitive problems, overcalls and many other valuable concepts are covered in depth. Increase your accuracy with the proven methods which have won numerous National titles and have been adopted by a diverse group of champions.
Published October, 1982
Recommended for: intermediate through expert.
ISBN 0-910791-02-3 paperback

THE COMPLETE BOOK OF OPENING LEADS
by Easley Blackwood
$12.95

An impressive combination: the most famous name in bridge has compiled the most comprehensive book ever written on opening leads. Almost every situation imaginable is presented with a wealth of examples from world championship play. Learn to turn your wild guesses into intelligent thrusts at the enemy declarer by using all the available information. Chapters include when to lead long suits, dangerous opening leads, leads against slam contracts, doubling for a lead, when to lead partner's suit, and many others.
Published November, 1982.
Recommended for: beginner through advanced.
ISBN 0-910791-05-8 paperback

THE BEST OF DEVYN PRESS
Bridge Books

A collection of the world's premier bridge authors have produced, for your enjoyment, this wide and impressive selection of books.

TEST YOUR PLAY AS DECLARER, VOLUME 2
by Jeff Rubens and Paul Lukacs
$5.95

Two celebrated authors have collaborated on 100 challenging and instructive problems which are sure to sharpen your play. Each hand emphasizes a different principle in how declarer should handle his cards. These difficult exercises will enable you to profit from your errors and enjoy learning at the same time.
Published October, 1982.
Recommended for: intermediate through expert.
ISBN 0-910791-03-1 paperback

TABLE TALK
by Jude Goodwin
$5.95

This collection of cartoons is a joy to behold. What Snoopy did for dogs and Garfield did for cats, Sue and her gang does for bridge players. If you want realistic, humorous view of the club and tournaments you attend, this will brighten your day. You'll meet the novices, experts, obnoxious know-it-alls, bridge addicts and other characters who inhabit that fascinating subculture known as the bridge world.
Recommended for: all bridge players
ISBN 0-910891-04-X paperback

THE CHAMPIONSHIP BRIDGE SERIES

In-depth discussions of the mostly widely used conventions…how to play them, when to use them and how to defend against them. The solution for those costly partnership misunderstandings. Each of these pamphlets is written by one of the world's top experts. **Recommended for: beginner through advanced.**
95 ¢ each, Any 12 for $9.95, All 24 for $17.90

VOLUME I [#1-12]
PUBLISHED 1980

1. Popular Conventions by Randy Baron
2. The Blackwood Convention by Easley Blackwood
3. The Stayman Convention by Paul Soloway
4. Jacoby Transfer Bids by Oswald Jacoby
5. Negative Doubles by Alvin Roth
6. Weak Two Bids by Howard Schenken
7. Defense Against Strong Club Openings by Kathy Wei
8. Killing Their No Trump by Ron Andersen
9. Splinter Bids by Andrew Bernstein
10. Michaels' Cue Bid by Mike Passell
11. The Unusual No Trump by Alvin Roth
12. Opening Leads by Robert Ewen

VOLUME II [#13-24]
PUBLISHED 1981

13. More Popular Conventions by Randy Baron
14. Major Suit Raises by Oswald Jacoby
15. Swiss Team Tactics by Carol & Tom Sanders
16. Match Point Tactics by Ron Andersen
17. Overcalls by Mike Lawrence
18. Balancing by Mike Lawrence
19. The Weak No Trump by Judi Radin
20. One No Trump Forcing by Alan Sontag
21. Flannery by William Flannery
22. Drury by Kerri Shuman
23. Doubles by Bobby Goldman
24. Opening Preempts by Bob Hamman

DEVYN PRESS
151 Thierman Lane
Louisville, KY 40207
(502) 895-1354

OUTSIDE KY. CALL TOLL FREE
1-800-626-1598
FOR VISA / MASTER CARD
ORDERS ONLY

ORDER FORM

Number
Wanted

_____ DO YOU KNOW YOUR PARTNER?, Bernstein-Baron .... x $ 1.95	=	_____
_____ COMPLETE BOOK OF OPENING LEADS, Blackwood .... x 12.95	=	_____
_____ HAVE I GOT A STORY FOR YOU!, Eber and Freeman .... x 7.95	=	_____
_____ THE FLANNERY TWO DIAMOND CONVENTION, Flannery ..... x 7.95	=	_____
_____ TABLE TALK, Goodwin .... x 5.95	=	_____
_____ THE ART OF LOGICAL BIDDING, Gorski .... x 4.95	=	_____
_____ INDIVIDUAL CHAMPIONSHIP BRIDGE SERIES (Please specify) . x .95	=	_____
_____ BRIDGE CONVENTIONS COMPLETE, Kearse (Paperback) .... x 17.95	=	_____
_____ BRIDGE CONVENTIONS COMPLETE, Kearse (Hardcover) .... x 24.95	=	_____
_____ 101 BRIDGE MAXIMS, Kelsey .... x 7.95	=	_____
_____ DYNAMIC DEFENSE, Lawrence .... x 9.95	=	_____
_____ PARTNERSHIP UNDERSTANDINGS, Lawrence .... x 2.95	=	_____
_____ PLAY BRIDGE WITH MIKE LAWRENCE, Lawrence .... x 9.95	=	_____
_____ WINNING BRIDGE INTANGIBLES, Lawrence and Hanson ...... x 2.95	=	_____
_____ TICKETS TO THE DEVIL, Powell .... x 5.95	=	_____
_____ PLAY THESE HANDS WITH ME, Reese .... x 7.95	=	_____
_____ BRIDGE: THE BIDDER'S GAME, Rosenkranz .... x 12.95	=	_____
_____ MODERN IDEAS IN BIDDING, Rosenkranz-Truscott .... x 9.95	=	_____
_____ TEST YOUR PLAY AS DECLARER, VOL. 1, Rubens-Lukacs ...... x 5.95	=	_____
_____ TEST YOUR PLAY AS DECLARER, VOL. 2, Rubens-Lukacs ...... x 5.95	=	_____
_____ DEVYN PRESS BOOK OF BRIDGE PUZZLES #1, Sheinwold .... x 4.95	=	_____
_____ DEVYN PRESS BOOK OF BRIDGE PUZZLES #2, Sheinwold .... x 4.95	=	_____
_____ DEVYN PRESS BOOK OF BRIDGE PUZZLES, # 3, Sheinwold ...... x 4.95	=	_____
_____ STANDARD PLAYS OF CARD COMBINATIONS FOR CONTRACT		
BRIDGE, Truscott, Gordy and Gordy .... x 5.95	=	_____
_____ PARTNERSHIP DEFENSE, Woolsey .... x 8.95	=	_____
_____ MATCHPOINTS, Woolsey .... x 9.95	=	_____

QUANTITY DISCOUNT
ON ABOVE ITEMS:
10% over $25, 20% over $50

We accept checks, money
orders and VISA or MASTER
CARD. For charge card
orders, send your card number and expiration date.

SUBTOTAL [   ]

LESS QUANTITY DISCOUNT [   ]

TOTAL [   ]

_____ THE CHAMPIONSHIP BRIDGE SERIES

VOLUME I .... x $9.95 (No further discount) [   ]

_____ THE CHAMPIONSHIP BRIDGE SERIES

VOLUME II .... x 9.95 (No further discount) [   ]

_____ ALL 24 OF THE CHAMPIONSHIP

BRIDGE SERIES .... x 17.90 (No further discount) [   ]

ADD $1.00   TOTAL FOR BOOKS [   ]
SHIPPING   SHIPPING ALLOWANCE [   ]
PER ORDER   AMOUNT ENCLOSED [   ]

NAME _____

ADDRESS _____

CITY _____ STATE _____ ZIP _____